COOKING WITH THE SUN

by Beth and Dan Halacy

MORNING SUN PRESS

Publisher: Jack Howell

Cover design and electronic publishing: Kathleen Gadway

Morning Sun Press

P.O. Box 413

Lafayette, CA 94549

phone & fax (510) 932-1383

Library of Congress Cataloging-in-Publication Data

Halacy, Beth
    Cooking with the Sun / by Beth Halacy and Dan Halacy.
      p. cml.
    Rev. ed. of: The Solar Cookery Book. 1978.
  ISBN 0-9629069-2-1
    1. Solar cookery. 2. Solar ovens. I. Halacy, D. S. (Daniel Stephen),
  1919- . II. Halacy, Beth. Solar cookery book. III. Title.
  TX834.5.H35 1992   92-3248
  641.5'8--dc20   CIP

Printed on recycled, acid-free paper.

Printed in the United States of America

Individual copies: $9.95 plus $2.00 postage and handling. Discounts available for quantity orders.

Morning Sun Press books are available at quantity discounts when used to promote products or services. For information please write to Premium Marketing Department, Morning Sun Press, 1240 Quandt Road, Lafayette, CA 94549, phone & fax (510) 932-1383.

We dedicate this book to

our wonderful daughters and their families.

ACKNOWLEDGEMENTS

Dan thanks his good friend Herb Wade for the many fine drawings in the book and aerospace engineer Glen Goodwin who helped get our oven temperature way up there!

Beth is specially indebted to her dear friend, Coralee Woody, who not only shared several of her wonderful recipes, but also took a solar oven home and tested recipes. Other fine cooks who have given Beth recipes or help for this book include Peggy Akin, Jay Blackshaw, Deirdre Byerly, Joe Costion, Jessica Fernandez, Helen Good, Jean Goodwin, Helios, Edith Hill, Dee Latimer, Loretta Larson, Jessica Koory, Betty Miller, Bonnie Peplow, Bess Rice, Mary Saylor, Bob and Janet Steelman, and Laura Woods.

Twenty years ago we used the Umbroiler, one of the first solar cookers available, to cook in an area where fire building was prohibited. We have developed our own cookers since then and often use solar energy to cook our food.

PREFACE

We cooked our first solar meal more than thirty years ago, shortly after attending the First World Symposium on Solar Energy in Phoenix, Arizona. Since then we've continued to experiment with the sun's energy. An earlier book of Dan's described a number of easy-to-build solar projects, including solar cookers. *Cooking With the Sun* is entirely about solar cooking, and describes in detail how you can make your own solar oven and reflector hot plate, and how to cook with them. Plus 100 tested recipes you'll enjoy.

Commercial solar cookers are expensive, but the two we show you how to build in this book are not. In fact, if you're a good scrounger you may be able to build them for little cash outlay! Best of all, both projects can be built by amateurs. Neither of us qualify as craftsmen, but our solar cookers work very well. Some of the tougher parts of construction we simply "farmed out" to the local sheet metal shop.

The potential of solar cooking is almost unlimited. How about solar brewed coffee? Or sun-cooked bacon and eggs? Steak or turkey? We can cook a turkey in the solar oven as fast as our electric oven can do it!

The first part of our book tells and shows you how to make the solar oven and solar hotplate. The second consists of the recipes Beth has tested over the years on both of them. You'll be able to cook entire meals—from soup to dessert—with sunshine!

Cooking With the Sun will appeal especially to solar enthusiasts but was written with **all** cooks in mind. As more cooks discover how easy and enjoyable solar cooking is, it will become more popular. Over the years we've learned that it appeals to many kinds of people:

- Those with an interest in conservation and the wise use of our resources, plus a desire to protect the environment.

- Campers who want to cook safely in wooded areas without the need for a fire, or the nuisance of waiting for that fire to get going. No smoke, no ashes. Just clean, hot heat!

- Backyard barbecuers and cookout specialists.

- Health advocates seeking more ways to put their ideals to practical use.

And of course *Cooking With the Sun* is for those who appreciate the fun and excitement of a new way of preparing food.

Perhaps you're already a solar chef; we hope that's the case. Our recipes and cooking tips will be just as useful with other solar ovens and reflector cookers. We hope that you'll like our book—and that most of your days will be sunny enough for your recipes to turn out well!

1

A BRIEF HISTORY
OF SOLAR COOKERS

It's easy to understand why solar cookers were experimented with two centuries ago. The sun had long been used for drying timber, hay, and other crops, so it was natural that humans also put food out in the sun to "cure" or dry. As science came into being, the men who studied it quickly learned the tremendous heat energy of the sun. A German physicist named Tschirnhousen, who lived from 1651 to 1708, reportedly used a large lens to focus the sun's rays and boil water in a clay pot. These experiments were recorded in studies of solar cookers published in 1767 by a Swiss scientist, Horace de Saussure. In studying the differences in air temperatures at high elevations and closer to sea level, de Saussure realized that Earth's atmosphere served as a heat trap for solar energy, causing higher temperatures at lower elevations, instead of the other way around as he had first expected. Coincidentally, he discovered that the wooden "hot boxes" he built for that purpose got hot enough to cook fruit.

French scientist Ducarla, a contemporary of de Saussure's, improved on these primitive solar hot boxes by adding mirrors to reflect more light into the box. He also insulated them and used five layers of glass instead of one to cover the box. Ducarla was on the right track, because he was able to cook foods, including meat, in just one hour. The British were interested by now, and Sir John Herschel used a more sophisticated, mirror-lined solar cooker during a scientific expedition to the Cape of Good Hope in South Africa.

August Mouchot, a French scientist who lived until 1911, wrote the first book on the subject, *Solar Energy and its Industrial Applications.* He was specially interested in solar cookers and called his favorite one, "The Solar Pot." He baked bread in about 3 hours and even built a solar cooker that steamed vegetables. His only failed experiment was cooking shish kebab right at the focal point of a parabolic mirror. Mouchot complained that the flavor and smell were terrible and blamed the problem on the "chemical rays" of the sun. In 1877, Mouchot designed and built solar cookers for French soldiers in Africa. These performed so well he received a sizable cash award from the French government.

Not surprisingly, American scientists also got into solar cooking. Among the first was Dr. Charles G. Abbot, who was for a long time the Secretary of the Smithsonian Institution. Abbot built solar cookers in which the heat collector was outside in the sun but the cooker itself was in the house, with heat carried from collector to cooker by circulating oil. Dr. Samuel P. Langley, another noted scientist, made a large box cooker of wood and in 1884 cooked meals with it atop Mt. Whitney near Pasadena, California.

By the early 1930s, a new generation of French scientists had renewed the country's interest in solar cooking, and many cookers were sent to French colonies in Africa. India too was beginning to investigate solar energy as a substitute for the dwindling sources of wood and fertilizer fuels in that country. By the early 1950s, Indian scientists had designed and manufactured commercial solar ovens and reflector cookers. Unfortunately, the new technology wasn't accepted by those it was intended for and the new industry was short-lived.

Because of the fuel shortage in developing countries, solar cookers were also being developed by American scientists, including Dr. Maria Telkes at New York University and Dr. Farrington Daniels and others at the University of Wisconsin. Telkes designed and demonstrated insulated solar ovens capable of reaching temperatures above 350° F, and the Wisconsin researchers produced inexpensive aluminum reflector stoves.

It was about this time that the Association for Applied Solar Energy (AFASE) was formed and held its first conference in Phoenix, Arizona in 1955. Many practical solar ovens and reflector cookers were demonstrated at this meeting and received wide publicity. This resulted in an effort by the United States to introduce solar cookers on Indian reservations in the American Southwest, and also in rural Mexico. As in foreign countries, this effort was not successful.

Canada's Brace Research Institute and Volunteers in Technical Assistance (VITA) in the United States also sponsored programs to popularize solar cooking in developing countries. The United Nations was involved too, and its Food and Agriculture Organization tested Dr. Telkes solar oven and the Wisconsin reflector cookers. Both performed well, but it is obvious that non-acceptance by intended users was the result of unwillingness to adopt a new lifestyle, lack of money to buy solar cookers, and perhaps political problems as well.

On the bright side, the Association For Applied Solar Energy later became the International Solar Energy Society, with chapters in many countries, including the American Solar Energy Society (ASES) which held its annual meeting in Denver, Colorado in 1991. More than 1400 delegates from dozens of foreign countries attended the conference, which included sessions on solar cooker design, and demonstrations of these cookers in use.

Early solar cooking devices were bulky, heavy, and expensive. Suitable materials were limited and few people knew about putting the sun to work effectively. But modern technological advances and materials have made solar cookers practical. Solar cooking equipment can be bought or home-built. The result is that every day the sun cooks more hamburgers and turns out more full-course dinners!

There are many advantages to cooking with solar energy. Solar cookers are not a fire hazard and can be used safely in areas closed to fires. There's no fuel to buy, no smoke or other pollution, and no ashes to clean up. Best of all, using solar cookers is fun.

Solar scientist Dr. Maria Telkes demonstrates her solar oven.

2

SOLAR ENERGY
AND HOW TO COOK WITH IT

One of the best things about solar energy is that you don't have to be a scientist or an engineer to understand and use it. Just the same, it's a good idea to learn a few solar basics.

Without the sun there would be no gravitation to hold Earth in its orbit, no solar heat to keep us from freezing, no food to eat, and not even light to see by. Yet we take all this for granted, seldom recalling the tremendous power in the sun's seemingly gentle rays. For example, in just a few days the sun showers us with as much energy as there is in all the fossil fuels in the world! Thousands of times more solar energy reaches us than we get from conventional sources, including coal, oil, gas, and nuclear fuels.

Bright sunshine falling on a modest-sized house with about 100 square yards of roof area is equivalent to the heat energy in 17 pounds of coal or 15 gallons of gasoline. Converted into electricity at an efficiency of about 10 percent, that energy would produce about 7 kilowatts of electric power while the sun is overhead. A single acre of land in direct sunlight receives the equivalent of about 4000 horsepower; a square mile receives about 2-1/2 million horsepower! It's easy to understand why solar energy is receiving so much attention as a power source, but for now we'll concentrate on solar cooking.

TURNING SUNSHINE INTO HEAT

On a sunny day our solar oven sometimes reaches 400° F, hot enough to bake a loaf of bread with a nice brown crust. To produce this heat we use the simple principles of reflection, concentration, glazing, the greenhouse effect and absorption.

A mirror reflects light (and heat) from its surface. Properly arranged, mirrors concentrate those sunbeams in the solar oven. Remember how hot the inside of your car gets in the summer sun? That's the "greenhouse effect:" glass lets in solar heat but prevents most of it from escaping. Upholstery gets so hot it's painful to sit on, and a black steering wheel is too hot to handle. This is the process of heat absorption. The solar oven uses this important principle to cook food at much higher temperatures than the outside air.

Early in the morning or late in the afternoon the glancing rays of the sun are weaker. Fortunately, solar cooking equipment isn't hampered by the varying solar output during the day. The trick is to "track" the sun, by pointing the solar cooker directly at it. Even in northern latitudes where the sun is low in the sky, we can cook by aiming the oven at the sun.

Clouds block much of the solar energy, although even on cloudy days enough heat gets through to permit some low-temperature cooking. Strong wind cools the solar oven, so if possible place the oven where it is sheltered from the wind.

SOLAR GEOGRAPHY

In Arizona we had an abundance of sunshine—often more than we wanted! Some parts of the state get about 4000 hours of sunshine a year and solar cookers work exceptionally well. Air temperature isn't all-important either. Our solar cookers did very well in the winter, even when the air was quite cool. In Flagstaff (7000 ft.), which has very clear air most of the time, a solar oven or reflector stove may do as well or better than in Phoenix because of the clear air. The same is true for Colorado, where we now live, and other high-altitude states. So don't be fooled into thinking that if you don't live in the sunny south you can't cook with solar energy.

We used to consider the "solar belt" as between the 40th parallels of latitude, but after a visit to a solar conference in Winnipeg we changed our minds. Winnipeg is about 50 degrees north latitude, but solar cookers work there too.

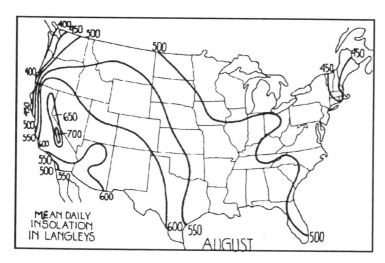

MEAN DAILY INSOLATION IN LANGLEYS   AUGUST

The map shows the amount of solar energy received in various parts of the country. Note that the areas with the least sunshine still get 75% as much as the sunny southwest.

3

BUILDING THE SOLAR OVEN

This do-it-yourself solar oven is much simpler to build than our earlier models. Constructed of plywood, window glass, and any of a variety of insulating and reflective materials, the oven can be completed in a short time by the average handyman or woman. We've even taught elementary school youngsters to make simple solar cookers.

Check the list of supplies and get together the materials you'll need for the oven. Perhaps you have scraps of plywood large enough for the oven—maybe even an old window pane that will do for the glass door. Reflectors can be made from cardboard boxes if you don't want to buy sheets of cardboard. Heavy-duty aluminum foil (the kind you wrap turkey in for broiling) will serve for reflective material to bounce additional heat into the oven, although aluminized mylar is more durable.

Read through the following directions before starting construction, and be sure you have all the materials and that you understand the building process.

List of Supplies Needed for Construction of Solar Oven

1 pc. plywood 3/4" x 16-1/2" x 17-1/4" (sides)
1 pc. plywood 3/4" x 16-1/2" x 18" (top & bottom)
1 pc. plywood 3/4" x 19-1/2" x 17-1/4" (back)
1 pc. plywood 3/4" x 6" x 8" (stairstep "angle adjuster")
8 sq. ft. 1" foil-covered fiberglass insulation
1 pc. double-strength window glass 18-7/8" x 18-7/8"
4 wood strips 1/8" x 3/8" x 20"
8 pcs. 1/16" thick aluminum or iron 1" x 4" (attachment angles)
4 pcs. cardboard, masonite, or sheet aluminum 18" x 18"
1 roll double-strength aluminum foil 18" wide
1 wooden drawer knob and attaching screw
1 fiber washer to fit drawer knob attaching screw
30 finishing nails 2" long
12 big-headed roofing nails 1-1/2" long
8 round-headed wood screws 5/8", #10
8 round-headed bolts 1/2", #10

8 nuts #10
8 1" washers, 3/16" hole
1 oven rack 8" x 12"
2 pcs. 1/2" wood dowel, 3" long
2 pcs. 1/8" brass rod, 15" long
1 sheet medium sandpaper
1 can non-toxic flat black paint

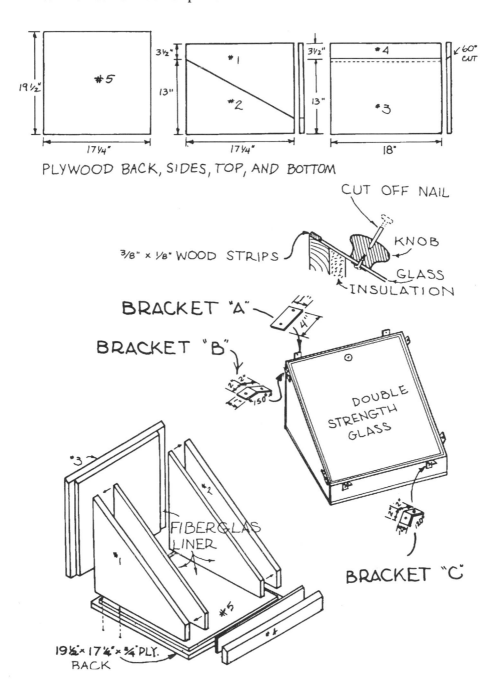

PLYWOOD BACK, SIDES, TOP, AND BOTTOM

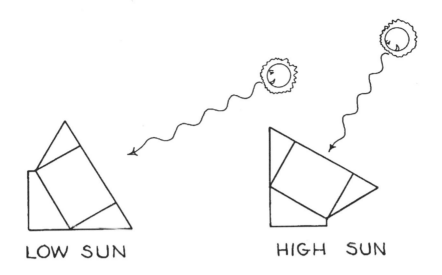

LOW SUN   HIGH SUN

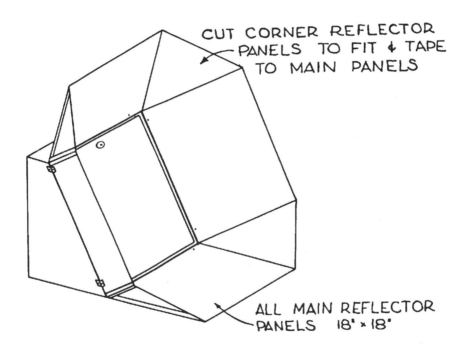

CUT CORNER REFLECTOR
PANELS TO FIT & TAPE
TO MAIN PANELS

ALL MAIN REFLECTOR
PANELS 18" × 18"

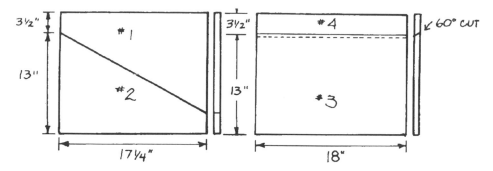

Layout for cutting the sides, top, and bottom of oven

THE OVEN BOX

Make the plywood body of the oven first. Note that the plans show a rectangle from which you cut both side pieces, and another rectangle for the top and bottom pieces. This saves wood and also makes construction easier. A table saw makes nice straight cuts but if you don't have one, don't worry. The oven shown in the photos was constructed entirely with hand tools.

SIDES—PARTS 1 AND 2

Be sure to cut the plywood rectangle that will form the sides accurately so that these parts will fit the top, bottom, and back pieces.

Now draw a line in the proper place to divide the rectangle into the two side pieces. Saw right on the line, using power tools if available. If not, clamp a straight board onto the plywood just on the pencil line. Hold the

Dan using the clamped board guide to help saw the sides accurately.

saw next to the guide and saw straight up and down. When you've completed the cut, the two pieces should match. Smooth the pieces with sandpaper and set them aside while you work on the top and bottom.

TOP AND BOTTOM—PARTS 3 AND 4

We used a simple method to save work in making the top and bottom pieces from the larger rectangle shown in the plans. Glue and nail the sides to the uncut piece, as shown in the photo. We put glue on one side, stood on the uncut top and bottom piece and held the side piece in place carefully, lining up the edges at the back of the oven. Nail with 2" finishing nails. Then do the same for the other side piece.

With both sides nailed to the uncut piece (it will stick out as shown in the photo), draw guide lines on both sides. Now saw carefully, frequently checking to see that you are following the guide lines. Take your time and make an accurate cut. The piece you have just cut off should fit neatly between the sides to form the top.

BACK—PART 5

Now you're ready to glue and nail the oven back to the sides. Apply glue and carefully nail the back to the already assembled sides, bottom, and top. Use 2" finishing nails. Keep all edges even so that the oven is square and true; then smooth it with a sandpaper block or sander so that the glass cover will lie flat on the open face of the oven.

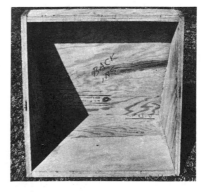

Left—The piece cut from the rectangle will become the oven top. Note the strip of wood holding sides together. Right—The completed oven box. Use wood filler where necessary to close up any gaps.

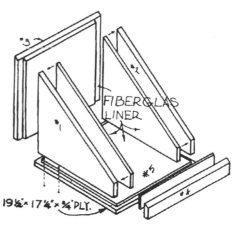

Left—Trim the aluminum part of the insulation after securing it with roofing nails, so that it can be easily stapled to the oven box. Right—Assembly of the oven box and fiberglass liner.

INSULATION

For an oven temperature of 250° F, we could stop right here. Instead, we add fiberglass insulation so that the oven will really heat up. We use Owens Corning/Fiberglas 704 Series rigid insulation 1 1/2" thick, faced on one side with tough aluminum foil, and get temperatures of 350° F and above. Check with your home supplies store for the insulation. The cost is low, and the material is easy to cut for fitting into the oven. Use a knife or saw.

Plan all cuts so that the aluminum side of the insulation will be on the inside of the oven and not up against the plywood walls. Fit the side pieces first. Trim one and use it as a pattern for the other—being careful to make them opposites so you get the aluminum foil on the inside. We tacked the insulation in place with the roofing nails. The fiberglass is soft, so don't drive nails in below the surface of the foil. Fit the top and bottom pieces and nail them in place. Then cut a piece for the back, push it into place, and nail.

Remember our discussion on a good solar energy absorber? Right now the shiny aluminum surface makes a good reflector instead. So paint it dull black. You can brush the paint on, or use a spray can. Be sure to buy paint labeled "non-toxic."

GLASS DOOR

The opening of your oven should measure 18" by 18". The double-strength window glass overlaps this opening 3/8" all around, so the glass must be 18-3/4" square. Have the glass cut at the glass shop unless you are experienced in working with glass. The glass shop can also sand the edges for safety and drill the 3/16" hole. The hole should be 2" from the edge and centered, as shown on the plans.

The small hole in the glass is for attaching the wooden drawer knob used for opening and closing the oven door. We bought a 1" wood knob and attaching screw and it worked fine. You may have to cut the end of the screw off with a hacksaw.

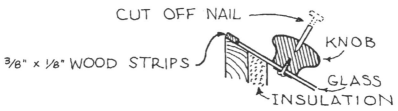

CUT OFF NAIL

3/8" x 1/8" WOOD STRIPS

KNOB

GLASS

INSULATION

Detail of oven door handle.

Also drill a small hole in the front center of the knob, as shown on the drawing. This should be a tight fit for a short length of nail from which the head has been removed. We inserted the nail by squeezing it and the knob in a vise. The nail should protrude from the front of the knob about 3/4". Round off the sharp edge with a file. This is a simple sun-tracking device—no shadow means the oven is pointing directly at the sun! Now attach the knob to the glass, using the fiber washer between the screw and the glass to guard against cracking.

To attach the glass cover on the front of the oven, place the thin wood strips all around, as shown in the plans and photo. To simplify this task, we used 1/8" x 3/8 x 36" balsa wood from a model airplane shop. We bought three pieces and used the cut-offs to piece together the fourth side. You can substitute balsa wood, pine, or other wood strips.

The wood stips are being glued to the oven face. The pins hold the strips in place while the glue dries.

As shown in the photo, block up the oven with the front face level. Lay the glass on it, with an equal distance from the glass edges to the outside of the box. Now apply glue to the strips of wood and carefully pin them in place, so they are not quite touching the glass. Don't let the glue run out from under the wood strips and touch the glass as this may cause you a little extra work getting the glass loose. Use quick-drying glue for this job and tack the wood in place with short brads.

Your solar oven will now work. In fact, this glass-covered box was all that early solar cooks used. On a good bright day the oven may reach above 200° without attached reflector panels. This temperature will do a great deal of cooking, but most times that isn't enough. So now we'll attach the shiny reflectors that bounce more solar energy into the oven.

Since light bounces off a mirror at the same angle at which it strikes it, we can attach a reflector the same size as the opening in our oven and reflect all the light striking it into that opening. But this is so only if we keep the reflector at an angle of 120° from the glass cover, as shown on the plan.

REFLECTORS

The reflector panels can be made from several different materials. Perhaps the simplest method is to cut 18" squares of corrugated cardboard and glue aluminum foil to them. If you do a smooth job, these will work almost as well as glass mirrors, and they are feather-light, cheap, and easily replaced if damaged.

We've had the best results using a double layer of cardboard. This prevents the reflector from warping as it tends to do when it gets damp or warm. (Remember, you'll need eight 18" squares using the double-layer method.) Apply a coating of rubber cement, white glue, or contact cement to the cardboard squares. Then press them together and lay them on a flat surface with a moderate weight holding them together until dry.

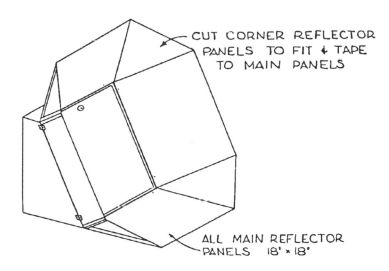

CUT CORNER REFLECTOR PANELS TO FIT & TAPE TO MAIN PANELS

ALL MAIN REFLECTOR PANELS 18' × 18'

Reflector panals attached and taped

With the cardboard squares dry and flat, you're ready to apply the reflective material. Be sure to use double-strength foil, in an 18" roll. It's possible to use thin foil, but heavy-duty is so much easier to use and keep smooth that it's worth the slight additional cost. We find it easier to apply glue to the cardboard and then place the cardboard on the foil, rather than doing it the other way. There's less chance of wrinkling the foil this way. Weight the cardboard and aluminum foil while they dry. Don't trim the foil until the glue has dried, and use a sharp knife.

We've also had good results making reflectors from 1" urethane foam with aluminum foil backing already attached. This home insulation material is very light and not expensive, and a 4-ft x 8-ft sheet made lots of reflectors. We've also used aluminized Mylar glued to thin masonite or other suitable backing material. Just about anything will work as long as you keep the reflector flat, smooth, and shiny. We buy aluminized Mylar on poster board backing from local art supply stores.

REFLECTOR ATTACHMENT ANGLES

The way the oven box is cut, the top and bottom reflectors require different angles attachments than the sides. So make sure all the angles are bent correctly or you'll be wasting solar energy and not cooking as well as you could.

For this reason, we had the angles bent at a sheet metal shop for accuracy and to save time. Aluminum is excellent; it should be 1/16" thick and not soft. If you cannot find aluminum, galvanized or black iron will do. Use 16 gauge metal. The angles are made from blanks 1" x 4" which are bent in the center of the 4" dimension. Because of the shape of the oven box, two fittings are left flat; four are bent to an open angle of 150°, and two are 120°. Make sure that the angles are exact so that each reflector will make the proper angle with the glass cover of your oven.

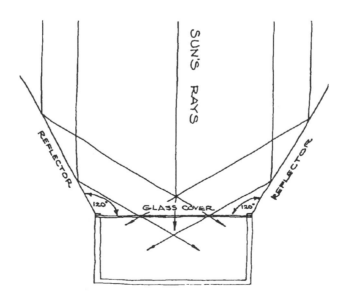

How the reflectors work.

Drill 3/16" holes in both ends of each attachment angle as shown on the plans. Clean the burrs from these holes with a slightly larger drill held in the hand, or with a knife blade you don't care too much about. Now you can attach the angles to the oven box. Hold an angle in place and line up its free leg with the face of the oven as shown on the plan. Mark through the hole onto the plywood for the location of the screw hole. To speed up the process, go ahead and mark all the holes now and do all the drilling at once.

Center punch the hole locations for accurate drilling. It will also help if you wrap a short piece of tape around the drill so you won't drill completely through the 3/4" plywood. About 5/8" is deep enough. Use #10 roundhead wood screws, 5/8" long. Tighten the angles in place, you are now ready to install the reflector panels.

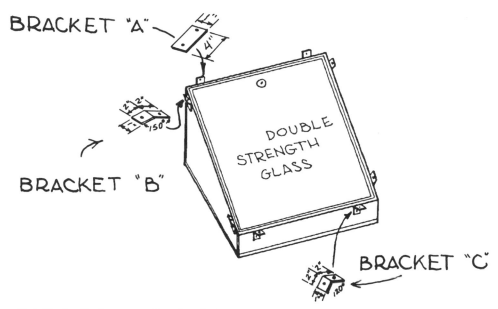

Detail of reflector mounting brackets.

Hold a reflector panel in place (with the aluminum foil toward the glass), just clearing the glass cover. Mark the panel very carefully with a pencil through the hole in the attaching angle. Again, you may want to use the mass production technique and mark all your panels at once.

We found the most accurate way to put the holes in the cardboard was to carefully force a punch or ice pick through the small pencil-marked circles, then run the 3/16" drill through the punched hole. When you have drilled all eight holes you are ready to mount the reflectors to the oven.

The reflectors are attached to the angles with #10 nuts and bolts, with a 1" washer under the bolt head on the reflector side. This large washer keeps the bolt from pulling through the soft cardboard. Attach all four reflectors, tightening the bolts snugly but not too tightly.

You are now doubling the amount of solar energy going into the oven, and its temperature will really soar. You can add even more heat by filling in the gaps between reflectors as shown in the drawings and photos. Cut four cardboard/foil triangles to fit into the gaps and tape them neatly in place with masking tape, duct tape or Velcro strips. Now your oven should reach between 300° and 350° on good days, enough to cook just about anything you want to cook!

The completed reflector oven with the triangles fitted into the corners.

For storing the oven when not in use, remove the glass cover, turn it over and replace it on the oven with the knob inside so that you can set the reflectors on it. For added convenience, you can hinge the reflectors to the oven with lengths of piano hinge.

Folding up the solar oven for carrying.

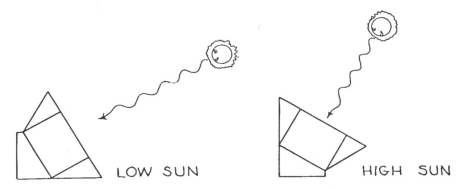

Using the low and high positions of the solar oven.

ANGLE ADJUSTER

Our solar oven has its glass cover angled at 60° so we can use the oven in two positions and thus point it at the sun more accurately for a longer part of the day. As the sketches show, for early morning and late afternoon cooking you tilt the oven to the lower position. This makes it point closer to where the sun is at those times. This "high sun—low-sun feature" is very helpful.

Even this improvement doesn't guarantee perfect aiming all day long, of course. So for those in-between times we added an "angle adjuster" with which you can easily point the oven at the sun so accurately that the sun's shadow disappears on the tracking knob. This sometimes gives high enough oven temperatures to brown the meringue on a lemon pie or do other high-temperature baking! Make the angle adjuster as shown in the plans, using 3/4" plywood. Then, as shown in the photo, raise the oven with one hand until it is aimed just where you want it. Then slide the stairstep in to hold it there.

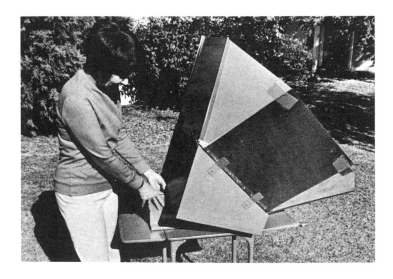

Beth using the angle adjuster to aim the oven at the sun. Note how the reflector panels are taped together.

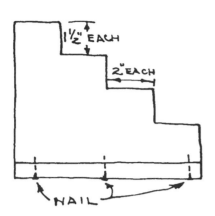

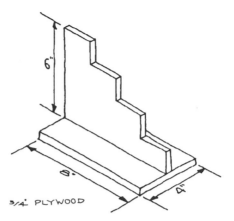

Solar oven angle adjuster.

OVEN RACK

We thought we had solved all our problems, until a casserole ran out of its tipped dish. So we added another feature: an oven rack that keeps the pan level no matter how the oven is angled. Starting with a rack bought in the household goods department, we had the sheetmetal man add wire hangers at each end, as shown in the photo and drawing.

The hangers fit over short length of aluminum tubing glued into holes drilled through the sides of the oven as shown. Using this handy accessory you can be sure a pie won't run out of the pan or a loaf of bread come out looking like it was baked on the side of a hill.

A little paint really dresses up the solar oven. Pick your favorite color and either spray or brush the outside of your creation a gleaming "solar yellow," "fire red," "flame orange," or whatever suits your taste. We painted the angle adjuster too. None of the colors will do anything for the temperature inside the oven but they make the outside more attractive. Ours was originally orange but now sports a brown leatherette trim on the outside.

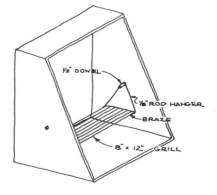

Swinging oven rack.

USING YOUR SOLAR OVEN

Your solar oven is now ready to use. Pick a sunny spot in the patio or back-yard (or even the front yard, if you like!) and set up for cooking your first solar meal. The oven works well right on the ground, or you can put it on a small table for more convenience and less stooping over. We sometimes put our oven on a table with wheels to make it easily movable.

The finger is pointing to the shadow on the knob. Adjust the oven until the shad-ow disappears; the solar oven will then be pointing directly at the sun.

Putting food in the oven is easy. Just open the glass door, put in the food, and close the door! An inexpensive oven thermometer should be standard equipment. This will let you know the oven temperature accurately—and it really impresses friends who can't believe a solar oven can get so hot!

Of course, you'll get the most solar heat by pointing your oven as directly at the sun as possible. The nail we put into the knob on the glass door is the suntracker that lets you aim the oven right at the sun. So check the shadow until it disappears and you'll be right on target. (You may see several faint shadows, but use the dark one.)

We have even learned how a meal can be cooked while you're away for several hours. The trick is to aim the oven at a point halfway between where the sun is at the start and the finish of cooking. This method works very well for a roast and vegetables. But a cake needs more exact focusing.

The inside of the oven gets very hot and the black paint may give off fumes and smell for a while. So leave the empty oven in bright sun for several hours until the smell is gone. Wipe any residue from the inside of the oven and the glass cover. When you're satisfied that the fumes and smell have burned off, you're ready to start cooking.

THE PORTABLE SOLAR OVEN

Around home it's easy just to leave the oven set up all the time. It's even a great conversation piece. Put some kind of cover over it to keep dust from the glass door and you won't have to clean it as often. Sooner or later, though, you'll want to take the solar oven on a picnic or even a camping trip. In assembled form it's rather bulky, so just remove the nuts and bolts and stack the reflectors against the glass door for a compact solar oven that travels. We installed a nice carrying handle on ours and this makes it even simpler to transport.

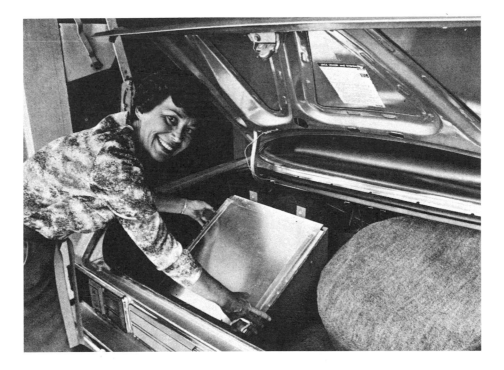

Beth can easily fit the folded-up oven in the small trunk of a compact car.

4

BUILDING THE
SOLAR HOT PLATE

You'll find that your solar oven handles a great variety of cooking tasks. But how about coffee or hot chocolate? Bacon and eggs, hot cakes, or even a juicy steak? This kind of cooking requires much higher temperatures, focused onto a much smaller cooking area. In short, we need a solar hot plate. Years ago we heard about a reflector stove made of cardboard by a man named Max Flindt, and the idea appealed to us. Cardboard is inexpensive, easy to use, and lightweight. So we tried one and it worked very well. The solar hot plate described in this book is the latest in a variety of different designs, sizes, and shapes that we tried. We think it's the best.

Our first reflector cooker was a giant, 48" in diameter. It cooked very well but was difficult to store and almost impossible to take anywhere unless we borrowed a pickup truck! After several generations of development, we realized that if the reflector was square instead of round it could be smaller in overall dimensions and still generate as much heat. This reflector stove is only 32" square but does an excellent cooking job.

List of Supplies Needed for Construction of Solar Hot Plate

3 pcs. cardboard 1/8" x 4' x 8' (reflector box and cover)
1 pc. pipe flange 3/4"
1 pc. pipe nipple 3/4", 4" long
1 pc. aluminum tubing 1/2", 24" long
8 sq. ft. double-strength aluminum foil or aluminized mylar
1 iron lampshade ring 5-1/2"
1 pc. iron rod 1/8", 6" long
1 pc. threaded iron rod 3/16", 2-1/2" long
l pc.wood l" x 2" x 35"
1 bolt 3/16" by 1-1/2" long
3 nuts 3/16"
1 sheet poster board
1 finishing nail
1 pc. heavy string 12"

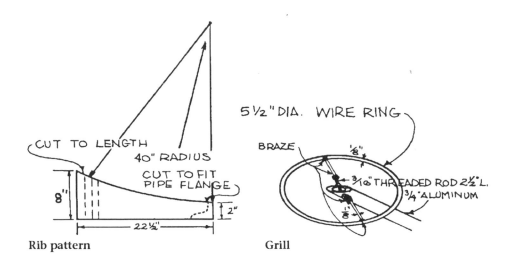

Rib pattern   Grill

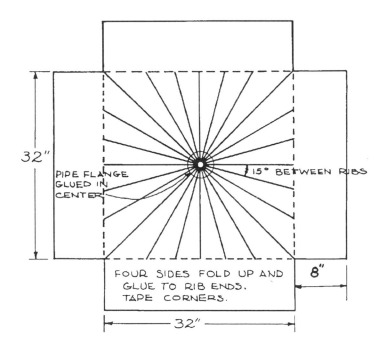

Layout of reflector box

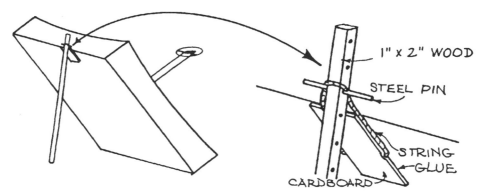

1" x 2" WOOD

STEEL PIN

STRING

GLUE

CARDBOARD

Reflector cooker support.

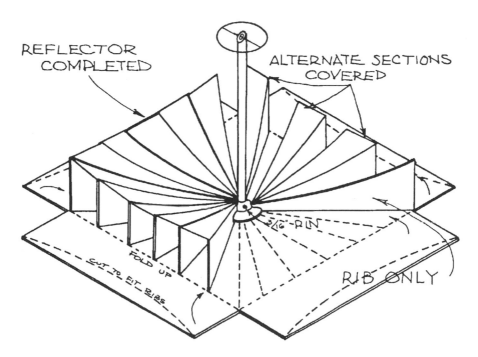

REFLECTOR COMPLETED

ALTERNATE SECTIONS COVERED

RIB ONLY

FOLD UP

CUT TO FIT RIBS

3/16" PIN

Hot plate assembly.

HOW THE SOLAR HOT PLATE WORKS

As kids, most of us used a magnifying glass to burn wood or leaves. A curved mirror does the same thing, concentrating all the sunlight that strikes it onto a tiny, very hot spot. Solar furnaces can be made in this way, and old searchlight mirrors are often put to such use. The parabolic curve of such a mirror results in very high concentration and temperatures of thousands of degrees! This would burn holes in a frying pan, of course, and we neither want nor need that powerful a mirror.

On our reflector we use the radius of a circle rather than a parabolic curve. We also form the mirror with a series of wedge-shaped pieces of flat reflective material instead of trying to mold them into a compound curve. This makes construction much easier and results in a hot spot about 6" square instead of a pinpoint. We've measured the grill temperature at more than 600 degrees F, so it really is a hot plate and must be treated with respect!

While the solar hot plate is easy to build, it does take some patience and care. Sloppy work will result in a solar cooker that won't get as hot as you'd like. So work slowly and accurately.

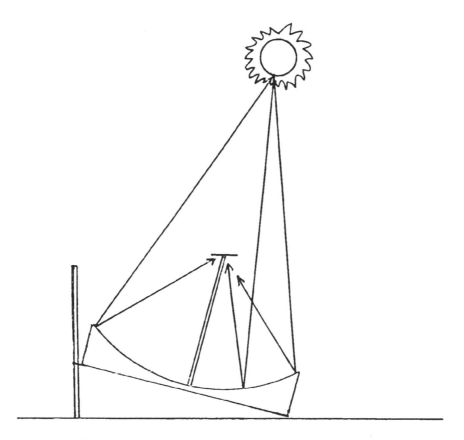

Solar energy reflecting to cooker hot spot.

CARDBOARD BASE

Start by carefully reading the directions and assembling the parts called for in the list of materials. You can buy 4-ft x 8-ft sheets of cardboard at a paper box factory, packaging store or scrounge used cardboard in sizes big enough for the cooker. Buy aluminum tubing at a hardware store, or search out bargains at a scrap metal place. Maybe you're even lucky enough to have the needed material right at hand.

Cut out the square cardboard base as shown in the drawing. Notch the corners and draw lines to locate the curve-forming ribs, making sure they intersect right at the center of the square. Draw the two diagonal lines first. Next, find the midpoint of each side piece and draw two more lines connecting them. With a protractor, divide each of the resulting 45° angles into three equal 15° angles. Twenty-four ribs times 15° equals 360°, a full circle. Draw all these lines, making sure they cross the center point.

Now turn the cardboard over and draw lines connecting the points of the corner notches. Very carefully cut through just one layer of cardboard, using a straightedge so the cut will be accurate. This makes it easy to bend the sides up when you reach that point in the construction—but don't cut all the way through!

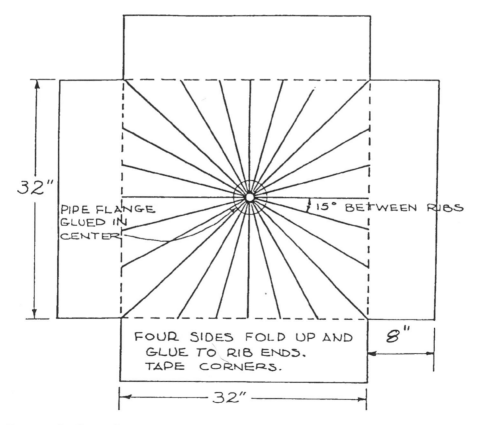

Layout of reflector box.

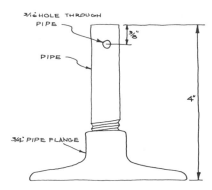

Detail of grill mount.

FLANGE ASSEMBLY

An important part of the cooker assembly is the flange that will support the cooking grill. Screw the 3/4" pipe nipple tightly into the 3/4" flange. Set the flange on a flat surface and measure up 4". Mark the pipe and then cut off the excess with a hacksaw, or have it done at the sheet metal shop. File the end smooth and clean out the inside of pipe so that the aluminum tubing will slide in easily. Now drill a 3/16" hole through the pipe as shown in the sketch.

The flange must be at the exact center of the reflector, so apply glue or epoxy liberally to its bottom surface and set it right over the intersection of the lines marking the rib positions. Make sure glue runs up out of the holes in the flange so that it will stick tightly to the cardboard.

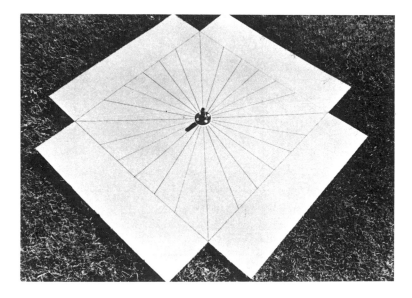

The reflector bottom has been marked for rib location and the sides have been trimmed. Note that the grill mounting flange has been secured with plenty of glue.

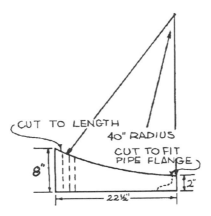

Layout of pattern for longest rib.

MAKING THE RIBS

Make the pattern for cutting the reflector ribs from the second cardboard sheet. As shown, draw a 40" radius beginning at a point 2" from the end of the cardboard sheet and right at its edge. Arrange the curve so that you will be cutting across the cardboard corrugations and not along them as this makes a much better cut.

Some careful craftsmen make a rib pattern of metal. Aluminum is a good choice because it is easy to cut. With such a pattern, it's easy to cut right along the edge with a knife or razor blade. However you make your pattern, cut it out carefully. On cardboard, use a sharp knife, linoleum cutter, or even a small hand saw. If necessary, sandpaper the pattern so that it's smooth and right on the line.

The master rib pattern is being made using a long strip of wood with a pencil inserted in a hole at the proper length.

Since the ribs cannot reach the center of the circle because the pipe flange is in the way, cut off an amount equal to half the diameter of the flange from the 2" end of the rib pattern. Trim a bit more from the bottom so that the pattern clears the base of the flange. Now place it on the cardboard square, snug against the flange, and mark the end of the longest, or diagonal rib. Make sure you get a vertical line here, and trim the pattern. Mark four ribs on the cardboard sheet, remembering to arrange the cuts across the corrugations as much as possible. Cut out these ribs carefully and set aside.

Now place the long rib pattern on the next shortest line on the base piece, with its small end right up against the flange. Make a vertical pencil line on the pattern to mark the end of the next shortest rib and trim off excess material with a razor blade or sharp knife. Now you have a pattern for another rib. Use it to mark out eight ribs. Cut these as you did the others and set them aside.

Move your pattern to the next shortest rib and mark its end. Trim off the excess and use the new pattern to mark out another eight ribs. After these are cut, move the pattern to the last rib and trim it off. You only need four of these so don't make too many.

You should now have 24 ribs in all. Remember to be accurate. Check the ribs against each other by setting them on a flat surface and holding the small ends even. The curves should match; if they don't the reflective material won't accurately focus the sun's rays on the grill. If necessary, do some more trimming or sanding so that the ribs all have the same curve.

The pattern has been traced on cardboard blanks which are all the same size. The pieces will be glued together so that the curves can be cut all at once.

One way to get very accurate ribs is to cut out two dozen rough blanks of cardboard large enough that you can trace the largest rib pattern on them. Glue all the blanks in a stack, putting glue outside the pattern so that the ribs will come apart later. Now cut the ribs on a bandsaw and all the ribs will have exactly the same curve.

RIB ASSEMBLY

We used model airplane glue (any quick-drying cement will do) so that we didn't have to hold the ribs in place very long. Make sure that the base piece is on a flat surface and does not curl up. You may want to weight it with bricks, paint cans, or something else to keep it flat until you get enough ribs in place. Put a glob of glue every 6" or so along the lines on the cardboard base and hold the proper rib in place until the glue has set. When all the ribs are glued in place, let them dry long enough for full strength. Overnight is best, if you have that much patience.

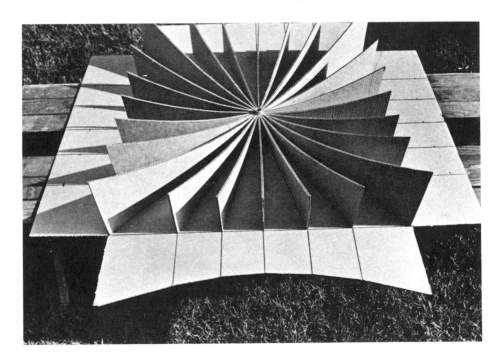

The ribs have been glued to the box and one side is trimmed and ready to be glued in place.

Now it's time to bend up the sides of the box and mark the top edges of the ribs so you can trim the sides in the gentle curve shown on the drawing and photos. This can be done by laying a strip of thin wood so that it touches all the points you have marked. Carefully trim off the excess with a knife or saw and prop up one side at a time for gluing. Use two or three big drops of glue on each side of each rib. When all four box sides are glued in place, prop the box almost vertical against a wall and add more glue, especially at the box corners and at center where the ribs touch the flange. Let the glue dry. This will make the reflector sturdy enough to survive an occasional hard knock.

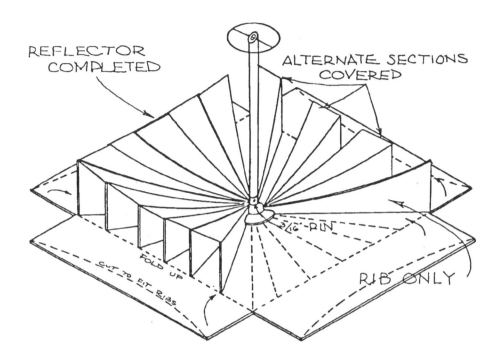

REFLECTOR COMPLETED

ALTERNATE SECTIONS COVERED

3/16" PIN

FOLD UP

CUT TO FIT RIBS

RIB ONLY

THE MIRROR FINISH

You have completed the skeleton of your reflector. Now it's time to add the curved reflector surface that will concentrate the sun's rays onto the cooking grill.

There are several ways to add this "mirror finish" to your reflector stove. Double-strength aluminum foil can be glued to poster board to make a durable, easily worked reflector material. Or you can use sheets of aluminized Mylar, or the aluminum-finish "Monokote" iron-on covering used for model airplanes. The Monokote makes the smoothest job, as our son-in-law in El Paso showed us. If you do use aluminum, coat the poster board with rubber cement and apply the foil very carefully to keep it smooth.

Make a pattern from poster board of the longest triangle needed. It should slightly overlap the two ribs it will cover. Use this pattern to mark three more poster board triangles. Then turn one of them over and mark four "opposite hand" triangles. This takes care of 8 of the 24 triangles needed. Now make patterns for the two other sizes of ribs—again making four right-hand and four left-hand so you can apply the reflective material to the same side of the poster board.

The complete reflector box has a circle of foil glued to the box where the narrow triangle ends meet. Note that the circle fits around the flange.

We found that the easiest way to apply the shiny triangles to the skeleton of the reflector is to first cover every other section, leaving openings between. Then apply the remaining triangles—always being sure you have the right one in each case. Use quick-drying cement applied to the edges of the back side of each reflector piece. Set the triangle in place and hold it down by hand or with weights until the glue sets. Carefully wipe off any excess glue before it dries.

You don't have to be too fussy in fitting the narrow ends of the triangles against the flange in the center. When all the triangles are securely glued in place, cut a 4" circle of poster board with aluminum material glued to it, cut a center hole, apply glue, and slip it down over the flange as shown in the photo.

When the glue has dried thoroughly, turn the reflector box over and apply masking tape to the outside joints. Except for a coat or two of whatever color paint you decide on, the reflector itself is complete unless you want to make a cardboard cover for it as shown in the photo. Be sure to make it big enough to fit over the reflector.

The completed cover fits snugly over the reflector box. Note how the reflector support holds up the box.

REFLECTOR SUPPORT

The 1" x 2" x 35" piece of wood is used to support the reflector at different angles to face the sun. Mark 12 holes on the 1" side of this support, as shown in the drawing. Start 1-1/2" from the top end and make the holes 1-1/2" apart. Drill them through the wood, using a drill that will just let the short length of 1/8" steel pin slide through. By positioning this pin in different holes, you can support the reflector at any desired angle

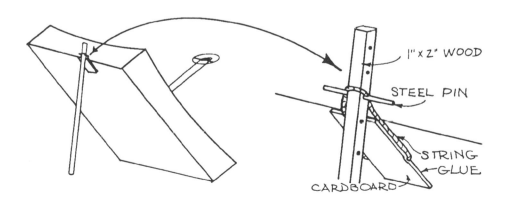

Construction of reflector support.

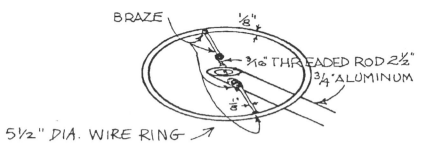

BRAZE — 1/8"

3/16" THREADED ROD 2 1/2"
3/4" ALUMINUM

5 1/2" DIA. WIRE RING ➚

Construction of hot plate grill.

THE HOT PLATE GRILL

Slip one end of the 1/2" aluminum tubing into the flange in the center of the reflector. If it's loose, wrap masking tape around the tubing until it's a snug fit. Because of the 40" radius curve of the ribs, the focal length of your reflector should be about 20". On ours we checked to make sure. To do this, insert the aluminum tubing in the flange and set up the reflector cooker so there is no shadow on it from the tubing. This means the reflector is pointing directly at the sun.

Now take a piece of wrapping paper about a foot square and cut a hole in its center large enough to slide easily over the aluminum tubing. Holding the paper at the edges, slide it down the tubing and watch for the bright spot that should be formed by your reflector. Move the paper back and forth until that spot is the smallest you can make it: this will be the focal point of your particular reflector cooker. Mark the point on the aluminum tubing, being careful not to burn yourself on the hot metal. Move the reflector out of the sun and when it cools cut the tubing to that length, which should be about 20". Now you're ready to install the cooking grill on the tubing.

The aluminum tube, with the grill mounted on one end, has been fitted into the pipe flange.

We bought a 5-1/2" diameter iron ring at the hobby shop. Normally used for making lamp shades, it's just right for our hot plate grill. Drill a 3/16" hole at the end of the 1/2" aluminum tubing as shown in the drawing, and insert the length of 3/16" threaded rod. Twist a 3/16" nut onto each side, and cut the two short pieces of plain 1/8" rod as shown on the drawing.

If you're not an experienced metal worker, have the brazing done at the local sheet metal shop. (We had ours done that way.) Take along the drawing so they will know what you need. Just be sure only one nut is brazed to the threaded rod. The other is left free so that it can be used to tighten the grill in a horizontal position no matter what angle your reflector cooker is tipped to face the sun.

You'll notice that the end of the aluminum tubing sticks up slightly above the surface of the grill. Saw or file off this excess metal at an angle, as shown in the drawing, so your pots and pans will sit level on the grill.

Now it's time to attach the lower end of the aluminum tubing to the flange so the grill won't twist and dump your coffee pot or frying pan. There are already screw holes in the flange assembly. Prop the cooker up on its support in a shady place so the sun won't be a problem. Carefully level the grill (use a level if you have one, or your good eyesight if you haven't) and hold it in place.

With an ice pick, reach through the holes in the flange and mark the aluminum tubing. Remove the tubing, make sure you have two marks, and then center punch the middle of the penciled circles. Drill 3/16" holes, one from each side. Then carefully run the drill two through both sides of the tubing at once. Re-insert the aluminum tubing in the flange and see if a 3/16" bolt will go through. If not, you may have to enlarge the holes in the tubing a bit with a slightly larger drill or a small round file. Slide the bolt into place, tighten the nut, and you are about ready to use the grill.

The hot spot is *very* hot and you'll want to keep your hands out of that area. So how are you going to tighten the grill in the level position? What we do is stand in front of the cooker to shade most of it and thus reduce the heat. Another method is to turn the cooker away from the sun, keeping it at the proper tilt, and then tighten the grill. The hot spot is very bright too, so wear dark glasses while working with the solar hot plate.

COOKING WITH SUNSHINE

The solar hot plate differs from your kitchen stove. It's lots more fun, for one thing. It also uses a moving source of heat, which makes cooking more interesting. As the sun moves, so does the focal point of your hot plate. Ideally, the reflector should point right at the sun (you can tell this from the shadow of the grill on the reflector), but you don't have to stand by every minute to move it. For some cooking tasks you can position the hot plate once and forget it. For others, you may want to move it every 15 minutes or so to speed up the process.

One helpful trick is to "lead" the sun a little. With experience, you'll learn how fast the shadow of the grill moves across the reflector. To get the most heat, aim the cooker ahead enough of the sun so it will be aimed right at the sun about midway through the cooking period. This guarantees the fastest cooking time if you don't want to move the cooker during the cooking period.

Sometimes the sun's movement can be helpful. For example, to cook soup and then keep it warm for later eating, just leave the stove in one position; the sun does the rest by moving. Your solar hot plate has a built-in automatic timer!

Try this technique: when you finish cooking something for an evening meal, leave the hot plate set up where it is. Next day, put food on an hour or so ahead of time and then go about your business. At the proper time, the sun moves into the right position, the hot plate heats up, and dinner cooks! Some campers use this technique with the morning coffee: they leave the hot plate pointing at the next day's early morning sun, prepare the percolator, and go to bed. Next morning they awake to the sounds, sights, and smells of fresh coffee perking.

The solar hot plate has limitations, of course. Since it's a concentrating mirror it uses only the direct rays of the sun and works best on a bright clear day; take it along next time you go to the mountains and you'll notice a big difference in the clear, thin mountain air! On cloudy or hazy days, there's less direct radiation and your solar stove will not perform as well.

A length of 2" by 4" board, placed on top of the box, keeps a pot of beans from upsetting the reflector.

As with the solar oven, the amount of radiation reaching the solar cooker depends on the position of the sun. When the sun is low its rays come through more smoke, dust, and other pollution that screens the direct rays. So you'll cook hotter and faster at noon than at 9 A.M. or 5 P.M. You can cook at those hours too by allowing more time to get the job done.

Because the reflector will be almost upright, be sure you don't put too much weight on the grill and tip everything over! When using the stove in early morning or late in the day, you may have to add some weight to the top of the reflector to keep it from tipping. As shown in the photo, we use a piece of 2" x 4" board about 30" long, or a pillow case partially filled with sand or small pebbles also works well.

TIPS FOR YOUR SOLAR HOT PLATE

We quickly learned that flat black paint makes the best grill, pot, or pan cook even better. Spray paint the *outside* surfaces of your solar cooking utensils and they'll heat faster. Put them on the grill in bright sunshine before using them and the paint will bake on nicely. And you won't get a paint taste in your food. You may want to use some of the elegant black gourmet cookware now available in department stores.

Use pots and pans large enough to accept all the solar energy your stove reflects onto the grill. A big pot is generally better than a small one. For hot cakes, or for searing a steak or hamburger, we've found that a skillet with a thick bottom works well. It stores up extra heat and quickly transfers it to food when you put it in the pan.

For food that requires a lot of cooking, be sure to cover the pot to keep the heat in. Because the solar hot plate is not as sturdy as the kitchen range, we use aluminum utensils in most cases, although a small steel pot or pan isn't too heavy.

A slight accumulation of dust (and even grease, etc.) doesn't greatly reduce the cooking power of the solar hot plate. But clean the reflector once in a while for best results. A "tack cloth" available from a paint store is handy for removing dust quickly. Grease can be removed with warm water and detergent. Aluminized Mylar is very durable because of its tough plastic coating. If you have used aluminum foil on your reflector, use care in cleaning and handling so it will last a long time.

A word of warning: don't let your solar hot plate get wet, especially if you haven't painted it. Water and cardboard don't mix well, so keep the cooker out of rainy or damp weather.

A black solar coffee pot perks faster!

5

OTHER COOKERS

We think our solar cookers are great, and we hope you'll build them. But the tips we've given, and the many recipes we've tested, can also be used with other solar cookers. Check the listing for commercial solar cookers in the back of the book. We've used a number of them ourselves. Some are quite compact and suitable for camping trips where cooking needs are not so great.

COMMERCIAL COOKERS

Unfortunately our favorite commercial solar hot plate is no longer available. We bought our Umbroiler about 20 years ago and it still works, even though it's a bit frayed around the edges. The invention of Dr. George Lof, the noted solar scientist, it's named for the umbrella it was made from.

    The beauty of the Umbroiler is that it folds up like an umbrella. So even if it rains you can at least use it to keep dry! Easy to carry in the trunk of a car, or even slung over your back, the Umbroiler generates plenty of heat and will make coffee, cook hamburgers, hot dogs, steak, and soup. It heats water to do the dishes, too. So if you come across one, or one like it, don't hesitate to try it out.

Our 20-year-old Umbroiler still works very well.

The best commercial solar oven we've ever used has to be Sam Erwin's "Solar Chef." Based on a design by British scientist Sir William Herschel, and using real mirrors, it produced very high temperatures and would cook just about anything. For fun, Sam built a monster "Super Chef" twice the size of his standard model. We watched it cook 40 pounds of beef for a big solar dinner in Phoenix one afternoon.

We fitted our standard-size Solar Chef with a cover, so that after we cooked a meal in it we could eat right on top of it! A real conversation piece for back yard or patio, it was sizable and heavy, and not the kind of cooker you travel with.

In the back of this book we've listed distributors of manufactured solar cookers for those readers interested in buying one readymade. One of those organizations is Solar Box Cookers International, a special kind of solar venture dedicated to spreading the use of solar cookers not just in our country but around the world.

The Solar Chef oven is constructed of real mirrors.

THE SOLAR BOX COOKER

In America, we use only about 1% of our fuel or electricity for cooking. But developing nations use a far greater percentage, with as much as 80% of the forests in developing countries (90% in Africa and Asia) reportedly used as fuel for cooking. As a result, there is already a serious shortage of wood in many countries and the outlook for the future is even worse.

For decades, the United Nations, as well as national agencies, concerned private groups, churches, and individuals in the U. S. and many other countries have attempted to introduce solar cookers into Third World countries critically short of wood or other fuels for cooking. In the 1950s, for example, the U. S. Agency for International Development launched a campaign to introduce cheap reflector stoves designed by University of Wisconsin scientists into Mexico and other countries.

Many of the developing nations have themselves set up similar programs. Two major types of solar cookers have been used: factory-made parabolic types something like the Solar Hot Plate in this book, and low-temperature "solar box cookers" generally made from cardboard. More than 100,000 solar box cookers and 15,000 solar reflector stoves had been distributed in India by 1990. And almost 100,000 solar cookers have been manufactured and sold in China for use in rural areas. But even this seemingly large-scale effort is only a tiny fraction of what will be needed to make a meaningful impact on the global deforestation problem.

The situation remains so critical that in 1991 a California hardwood broker commissioned an in-depth study by researcher Darwyn O'Ryan Curtis on the feasibility of solar cookers as a possible solution to the problem.

Photo by Raven Wood

Solar Box Cookers International "Solar Box Cooker"

To the question, "could an American commercial enterprise contribute significantly to forest protection by promoting solar cooking at this time?" Curtis answered, "No." The problem seemed to boil down to the fact that affordable cookers aren't acceptable, and acceptable cookers aren't afford-able—a Catch 22 that has thus far delayed the vital saving of wood fuel. But Solar Box Cookers International believes there is hope.

The original solar box cookers were designed in the mid-1970s by Barbara Kerr and Sherry Cole in Arizona. These low-cost, low-temperature cardboard cookers can be used to slow-cook simple meals during the day. They can also be built with locally available materials and achieve tempera-tures of about 250° for cooking soups, vegetables, and meat—and also for sterilizing water.

It is estimated that billions of people are short of fuel for cooking, but getting them to accept solar cookers has met with limited success so far. Reasons given include slow cooking time, unfamiliar cooking methods, clouds stopping the cooking process, wind blowing cookers over, and lack of durability of the cookers.

However, the World Conference on Solar Cooking held at the University of the Pacific in Stockton, California in 1992 is indicative of the continuing interest in solar cookers for the developing world.

On page 109 we offer plans for building the "Minimum Solar Box Cooker", courtesy of Solar Box Cookers Northwest, 7036 18th Avenue N.E., Seattle, WA 98115

6

BETH'S INTRODUCTION
TO SOLAR COOKING

Thirty years ago when I started cooking with a solar oven and reflector stove, it was just a novelty. We liked to have friends, Boy Scouts, and others interested in solar energy come over to see how well we could cook with the sun. Occasionally we enjoyed taking these cookers along on a picnic or camping trip. And of course I traveled extensively to publicize our book, all over Arizona and California, with lots of TV and radio appearances. I flew to Chicago to help with a colossal turkey cookout at Governor's State University Fair in Illinois using two dozen of our ovens built by local solar fans! I guess the most exciting trip was the time I flew to Florida (taking along the oven and reflector stove) to appear on the Dinah Shore TV show. Even intermittent rain that made the solar cooking demonstration difficult didn't put a damper on that experience.

Today I cook with sunshine for a different reason. Since the energy crunch, my outlook changed from a once-in-a-while demonstration of a novel method of cooking to a potential way of life. Many friends told me they were excited about cooking outdoors, especially in summer when they didn't want to heat up the house. Some had cut down on baking in the summer months because of the expense of air conditioning. But solar cookery makes it possible to bake without heating up the house.

The recipe section is the result of my experience over the years with solar cookery. Many people have helped with recipes I've adapted for the solar oven and reflector cooker. These recipes, varied as they are, are only an introduction to what you can do with solar cooking. I really believe that just about any dish can be cooked this way.

Start with simple recipes to avoid problems. Many things are very easy to cook with the solar oven and reflector cooker, so don't try a difficult cake or gourmet meat dish first time out. Then, after a little practice, you can try your own favorites and experiment with solar cookery your way.

Read the following tips carefully before attempting to cook a meal with your new solar cookers. These helpful suggestions will familiarize you with the differences between conventional and solar cooking.

USING THE SUN

Locate the most sunny and wind-sheltered place in your yard or patio. When you get up in the morning and decide to cook with the sun, think not only of meal planning but also about what kind of solar day it is. If it's exceptionally clear and sunny, you might decide to do some extra baking—like a special cake. So go out and set up your oven and focus it so it will be hot and "ready to go" when you decide to bake bread, put together a casserole, or simply defrost something. Automatically *think solar!*

COOKWARE

You can use any kind of cookware with solar energy, but dark, lightweight cookware heats up faster. Shiny steel or aluminum pans are less efficient because they reflect heat away from the food. I do use my aluminum pans, which have been spray-painted black on the exterior for more heat absorption. However, one of my favorite pieces of casserole cookware is a heavy pottery dish. It takes longer to heat up, but once hot, it holds the heat better.

Don't use aluminum foil around your meat or vegetables, or as a cover for a casserole. The aluminum foil will reflect the heat away from the food. Use a Reynolds plastic oven bag, especially when cooking turkey.

FOCUS

Perhaps the biggest difference between your kitchen oven and your solar oven is that the heating element of the one in the kitchen stays still, while the sun, which heats your solar oven, is always moving. It moves slowly, but you'll have to remember to move the oven or reflector cooker occasionally to keep the heat where you want it.

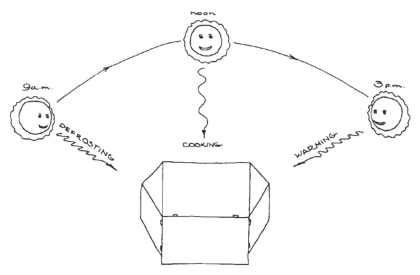

Using "automatic timing" with the solar oven.

The morning sun is very low in the sky, so aim your cooker low to catch its rays. The same is true in late afternoon, and sometime before sunset we are done with solar cooking because the sun is too low. Aiming the solar oven and reflector stove is done by watching shadows and is very easy. In a few days you'll be an expert on how fast the sun moves and how to adjust the oven for desired temperatures and best results. Remember that when there is no shadow from the nail in the oven glass knob, your oven is pointing directly at the sun.

You'll find that you can make use of the automatic timer offered by the sun's movement. With experience you'll be able to aim the cooker to point where the sun will be in a few hours. This will let you put food in the oven early, cook it, and then keep it warm for some time. You can even use this technique to defrost food and then cook food with one setting. See the drawing for a clearer picture of this method.

TEMPERATURES AND COOKING TIMES

Most of my recipes are planned to cook at approximately 300° unless otherwise designated. This is because it's sometimes difficult getting the oven up to 350°. However, most food, except some desserts, can be cooked at lower temperatures. Just leave the food in the oven longer. You'll find more specific instructions on timing at the beginning of each chapter.

Solar cooking is not the same as setting a thermostat and timing with a clock. At first you must watch more carefully and learn how long a recipe is going to take. For meats, the timing is about the same as on the kitchen stove. You can be sure by investing in an inexpensive meat thermometer. However, for bread, cookies, and cakes, you won't always have as high a solar oven temperature as in your gas or electric oven. Adjust the time accordingly, and you'll find you can cook just about anything. You really can bake cakes at a lower temperature than in the house. It just takes longer.

PRE-HEATING THE OVEN

It's usually best to pre-heat your solar oven before starting to cook, unless you're using your oven to defrost something first. It will take thirty to forty minutes for the oven to warm up, depending on weather conditions..

A 14-pound turkey cooks in 3 hours on a good day.

SUNGLASSES

Solar ovens reflect a lot of heat and a great deal of light. The reflection from the solar hot plate can be even stronger. I always wear sunglasses when cooking because of the light intensity. The glasses protect your eyes and make it easier to see inside the oven.

OVEN RACKS

We have a swinging rack to keep the food level when the oven is tilted for focus. And we recommend a cooking rack be used even when the oven is flat. As good cooks know, this allows heat to circulate under the food and cook it evenly.

SEASONS

Remember that in the winter the sun rises later and sets sooner. Also, it's lower in the sky even at noon. Wintertime direction is a constant low-in-the-sky focus. Just aim your solar cooker at the sun and it will do its job. You'll find that you have more solar cooking hours a day during the months of May through September. And because the sun is higher in the sky, you'll have a hotter oven. It's during these months that you will most enjoy cooking the high-temperature recipes.

THE GEOGRAPHY OF SOLAR COOKING

If you have a sunny spot in your yard, it isn't critical whether you live in Arizona or Maine. There can even be snow on the ground as long as the sun is shining brightly. The temperature of a solar cooker is determined more by the amount of sunshine than the outside air temperature.

When relatives from Utah visited us in Arizona, their reaction to my solar bread-baking was interesting. "Sure," they said, "it works here in Phoenix where it's hot, but it wouldn't work in Utah." They were so wrong! It could work even better in Utah where the air is clearer in the high altitude.

WORKING WITH THE WEATHER

Let's face it, there are times when the sun just doesn't cooperate. So don't get rid of your inside cooking equipment! Just consider it a "backup" to your solar cookers and use it when you have to. At the same time, don't always let cloudy weather chase you indoors. Clouds move and the skies may clear again; learn to work with the weather.

The solar oven is a combination reflector and flat-plate cooker. The plate part, the glass door, works well even under an overcast sky. I've cooked a roast and vegetables on slightly overcast days when I wondered if it was going to work, and I was amazed at the performance of the oven.

The solar reflector stove, on the other hand, must have a clear sky because it's like a big lens and won't work without the direct rays of the sun.

SOLAR HOT PLATE COOKING

For me, the oven is the workhorse of the cooking team. But for steaks, hamburgers, and hot dogs, plus breakfasts of bacon and eggs and hotcakes, the solar hot plate is a necessity. You won't believe it the first time you see, hear, and smell coffee perking or soup bubbling on it!

I use the reflector for cooking sauces and gravies, soups, lentils, beans, and other vegetables. And, of course, I use it for heating water for various purposes.

When the recipes say simmer, turn the reflector cooker slightly off focus so the grill won't be too hot.

Don't overload the grill. I use a lightweight 1-1/2 quart pan for cooking sauces, soups, beans, and the like, and an 8" frying pan for bacon, eggs, steak, and hamburger. These pans, along with our 6-cup coffee pot, have been spray-painted black on the outside for maximum heat absorption.

As described in Chapter 4, you can weight the hot plate down in the back to prevent tipping. Handled with care, it will perform well and last a long time.

Solar cooks, aged 8 and 9, frying eggs for breakfast.

COOKING SYMBOLS

The recipes keyed for "high sun" cook fastest and best on clear sunny days. For example, cakes and pies should always be cooked as close to noon as possible. "Low sun" recipes do well in the morning, late afternoon, and in wintertime. Some recipes can be cooked under either condition but may take much longer with low sun, or cook faster than you would wish with high sun. Recipes not keyed for either sun position can be cooked with either high or low sun.

 REFLECTOR COOKER

 SOLAR OVEN

 LOW SUN

 HIGH SUN

 OPTIONAL

7

BREADS

It may surprise you to know that the solar oven lends itself very well to baking bread. Two of the questions most frequently asked are, "Does bread brown, and are the rolls light?" The answer is "yes" to both. Just be willing to take as long as is needed to get the bread as brown you want it. One day I baked four dozen rolls for two hours. It was an overcast day and the sun kept popping in and out from behind the clouds, causing the temperature to vary greatly. But the rolls were light, brown, and delicious.

It has been said that many people have never tasted real bread. I refer to those who have eaten only "store-bought" bread and not experienced the enjoyment that comes from eating the home-baked variety. I consider nutrition when baking breads, so I use unbleached white flour as well as the other natural grains. Also, I substitute natural sugar, honey or molasses for the processed sugar often used in recipes.

When considering the amount of flour used in my recipes, remember that it's almost impossible to give an exact amount for each recipe because of the difference in the characteristics of flour, as well as variations in the weather. So when a recipe calls for kneading in extra flour, just knead in as much as you need to achieve a dough that is not sticky and has good consistency.

As with cakes, the middle of the day is best for solar bread-baking. The recipes in this chapter are planned for about a 300° - 325° oven. If the air is very clear and the oven reaches a higher temperature, all the better.

First, let your oven reach its maximum temperature. If 350° is maximum, the temperature will probably drop to around 300° or 325° as you put in the bread, muffins, or rolls. Then it may rise again slowly. Learn what the variables are, be a little adventuresome, and you'll become as addicted to baking bread in your solar oven as I am. It's really fun!

Your oven can also be used in wintertime as a place to let the dough rise. Simply turn the oven so that it's off focus and doesn't get too warm.

TIPS FOR BREAD RECIPES

1. If the recipe calls for sour milk, you can make sweet milk sour by adding 1-1/2 tablespoons of lemon juice or 1-1/3 tablespoons of vinegar to each cup of milk.

2. If you want a soft crust , simply brush the bread with butter while it's still warm.

3. When the recipe is for two loaves and you want to bake one loaf at a time, simply keep the second loaf in the refrigerator after it has risen the second time. Then let it return to room temperature and bake.

4. Keep dough out of a draft while it is rising.

5. Sourdough starter is usually obtainable at any gourmet shop. However, you can make your own. All you need is flour, sugar, water, and patience. To get your starter started, just put some flour, sugar, and lukewarm water together and let it sit on the back of your stove or somewhere else where it will remain at a fairly warm, constant temperature. It should not cook. A temperature of 80° - 90° F is about right.

   Eventually the yeast spores in the air will get into the mixture and start growing; thus beginning the process of fermentation. You can tell when it has begun by the bubbling of the mix and by the typical yeasty odor. The yeast organisms will, of course, be growing all the time in the mixture, so that after a while you have a bowlful of active yeast. Refrigerate the starter to keep it fresh.

   To keep the starter alive you must use a little every week. To replenish the sourdough starter add 1/2 cup of flour mixed with 1/2 cup condensed milk.

6. Remember that you can cook bread and rolls at lower temperatures if you adjust the cooking time accordingly.

QUICK AND EASY BEER BREAD

Since we first wrote *Cooking with the Sun,* our daughters have grown up and now rival me with their own cooking. Deirdre likes this recipe and shared it with me.

> 1/2 cup butter
> 3 cups self-rising flour
> 2 tablespoons sugar
> 12-ounce can beer

Melt butter and pour enough into a 9" x 5" loaf pan to coat the bottom. In a large bowl mix together flour, sugar, and beer. Spoon dough into loaf pan. Pour remaining butter over the top. Bake at 325° for 1-1/2 hours, or until bread is light golden color. Let stand 10 minutes before cutting. Makes 1 loaf.

TEXAS BISCUITS

I'll never be able to make biscuits like my mother did. There was just something about her touch. She told me that on the ranch when her brothers were out on a round-up, they mixed biscuits right in the top of the flour sack, not even using a bowl. She said to use two walnut-size-dabs of shortening for this recipe. As near as I can figure out, that would be about two tablespoons. Here is her recipe:

> 2 cups flour
> 3 rounded teaspoons baking powder
> 1 teaspoon salt
> 1 tablespoon sugar
> 1 cup milk
> 2 tablespoons shortening

Combine dry ingredients and cut in shortening. Make a hole in the middle of the dry ingredients and add milk. Work mixture into a ball and knead lightly, then roll out and, with a cutter dipped in flour, cut your biscuits. Dip each side of each biscuit in melted butter or oil and place on sheet pan. You can stack another biscuit on top and press ever so lightly together, or leave them single. Bake at 325° for about 40 minutes. Makes 2 dozen medium biscuits.

SOURDOUGH BLUEBERRY MUFFINS

> 1/2 cup whole wheat flour
> 1/2 cup white flour
> 1/2 cup sugar
> 1/4 teaspoon baking soda
> 1/2 teaspoon salt
> 1/2 cup vegetable oil
> 1/2 cup evaporated milk
> 1 egg

3/4 cup sourdough starter
1 cup fresh or frozen blueberries, raisins, or lingonberries

Mix together the first eight ingredients in order of their listing, adding enough sourdough starter to make the mixture moist and hold together nicely. Do not beat vigorously. Fold in the frozen blueberries very gently, to avoid turning your dough purple. Drop mixture into greased muffin tins; the cups should be half full. Bake for 40 minutes at 325°.umtil the muffins are a nice light-medium brown. Makes 18 medium muffins.

CEREAL MUFFINS

It's always fun to discover a good recipe when dining with friends and then find that it works well in the solar oven. This is a favorite.

1 cup all bran cereal
1 cup crushed shredded wheat
1 cup boiling water
1/2 cup shortening
1-1/2 cups sugar or 1 cup honey
2 eggs
2 cups buttermilk
1 cup quick oatmeal
2-1/2 cups flour
2-1/2 teaspoons baking soda
1-1/2 teaspoons salt

Combine bran cereal and crushed shredded wheat; cover with boiling water. Do not stir. Cool to lukewarm. Cream shortening, sugar or honey, and eggs. Add buttermilk and oatmeal to creamed ingredients. Sift flour, soda, and salt together; add to egg and shortening mixture. Add the cooled cereals, stirring briefly. Bake in muffin tins at 325° for 45-55 minutes. Makes four dozen muffins.

EASY BANANA SANDWICH BREAD

1/2 cup butter
1 cup sugar
2 eggs
3 crushed bananas
2 cups sifted flour
1 teaspoon baking soda
Pinch of salt
1/4 cup broken pecan meats

Cream butter and sugar; beat in eggs. Add bananas and beat well. Mix in flour, soda, and salt. Stir in nuts. Pour into greased 9" x 5" x 3" pan and bake 1 hour at 300°-325°. Makes one loaf.

MEXICAN SPOON BREAD

This is a moist spoon bread that is served with a tomato sauce over the top. With a tossed salad and a vegetable it can be a main course.

Bread
1-pound can cream style corn or 3 ears of fresh, uncooked corn
1 cup corn meal
1/3 cup melted shortening
2 eggs, slightly beaten
1 teaspoon salt
1/2 teaspoon baking soda
4 freshly roasted chilis, chopped
   (reserve 1/3 for the sauce)
1-1/2 cups shredded cheddar cheese

Combine the first five ingredients and mix well. When using the fresh corn, simply scrape the kernels from the corn cobs and combine with remaining ingredients. Pour half of the batter into a greased 8" square pan. Sprinkle with green chilis and half of the cheese. Pour the remaining batter on top and sprinkle with the other half of the cheese; bake for about 1 1/2 hours at 300°-325°.

Sauce
3 or 4 fresh tomatoes, chopped
1/2 cup tomato juice
reserved chopped green chilis
1 teaspoon salt pepper
1/4 teaspoon oregano
2 tablespoons chopped fresh cilantro

Chop the tomatoes until they are chunky. Combine with the remaiing ingredients and simmer on the reflector grill for about 1/2 hour. Pour the sauce over the baked bread. Makes 6 - 8 servings.

OLD-FASHIONED CORNBREAD

2 cups corn meal
2 cups sour milk or buttermilk
1 teaspoon baking soda
1 tablespoon sugar
2 tablespoons shortening, melted
1 teaspoon salt
1 egg

Mix dry ingredients. Add milk, beaten egg, and shortening. Pour into 8" square pan and bake for 40 minutes at 300°. Makes one 8" square bread.

LIGHT ROLLS

One of the breads that makes a big hit with our family is just a plain light roll. Remember that dough for rolls is softer than for plain bread, as soft as can be handled without sticking to hands or board. Once I learned that rolls require only thorough mixing, with little or no kneading, I began to have a lot more success with roll-making.

> 1 cup milk, scalded
> 2 tablespoons shortening
> 2 tablespoons sugar
> 1 teaspoon salt
> 1 cake fresh or 1 package dry yeast
> 1/4 cup lukewarm water
> 1 egg
> 3 cups flour

Combine milk, shortening, sugar, and salt; cool to lukewarm. Add yeast softened in lukewarm water. Beat the egg well and add to mixed ingredients. Beat vigorously; cover and let rise in warm place (80° - 90°) until doubled in bulk, about 2 hours. Turn out on lightly floured surface and shape into your preferred shape for rolls. I like to shape 2" balls, flatten and roll them, and place them in the pan. Let rise until double in size again. Then bake at 300°-325° until nice and brown on top. Makes 2 dozen rolls.

HELEN'S WHEAT BREAD

> 1 package dry yeast
> 1/2 teaspoon sugar
> 1/4 cup lukewarm water
> 1 cup lukewarm water with 4 tablespoons melted margarine or butter
> 1 egg, beaten
> 1 tablespoon salt
> 1/4 cup sugar or 2 tablespoons honey
> 1-1/2 cups white flour
> 2 cups wheat flour

Mix yeast, 1/2 teaspoon sugar, and 1/4 cup water; let stand 10 minutes. Combine water and butter, egg, salt, sugar or honey; add to yeast mixture. Add 1-1/2 cups white flour and beat well. Slowly add wheat flour, beating well. Knead the bread until it is smooth (about 10 minutes). Place dough in a large, well-oiled bowl and turn it so that it is oiled on all sides. Let rise until double in bulk (about 1-1/2 hours). Punch down and form into 2 loaves and put into oiled bread pans to rise until double in size again. Bake at 325° for about 55 minutes. The bread is done when it sounds hollow when tapped on the top. Makes one large loaf.

CORNELL BREAD

The woman who gave me this recipe said it is so nutritious that she can have a couple pieces of toast from this bread in the morning with a glass of orange juice, play eighteen holes of golf, and have energy to spare!

    3 packages of dry yeast
    3 cups warm water
    1/3 cup molasses
    1-2/3 tablespoons vegetable oil
    5 cups whole wheat flour, sifted
    5 tablespoons soy flour
    7-1/2 ounces non-fat dry milk
    4 tablespoons wheat germ
    2-1/2 tablespoons brewer's yeast
    2 tablespoons salt

Mix yeast, water, and molasses; let stand 5 minutes. Add 1-2/3 tablespoons oil to yeast mixture. Combine remaining ingredients and stir into yeast mixture. The dough will be sticky. Turn onto a floured board and knead until smooth, adding flour as needed. Turn into greased bread tins and let rise. The dough is heavy, so will not double in size. Bake at 325° - 350° for 1 hour and 15 minutes. Makes 2 loaves.

FRENCH-ITALIAN BREAD

This is probably the most simple white bread recipe ever devised. It also happens to be our favorite, and we never tire of it.

    1 package active dry yeast
    1 cup warm water (110°F)
    1-1/2 teaspoons sugar
    1 teaspoon salt
    2 - 3 cups flour
    1/4 cup corn meal

Dissolve the yeast in water in large bowl. Add sugar, salt, and 1 cup of flour. Beat until thoroughly blended. Gradually stir in the remaining flour until the batter is quite stiff. Then knead in amount of flour necessary to make a nice smooth dough. Knead for ten minutes and then turn into a well-oiled bowl, turning so that the dough is oiled all over. Cover and let rise for 90 minutes or until double in size. Punch down, remove from bowl, and let stand on floured board for 10 minutes. Form into a long loaf. Place on a greased cookie sheet dusted with corn meal. Slash top of loaf diagonally. (You can also form a regular loaf and place it in an oiled bread pan). Let rise 90 minutes. Bake for about 45 minutes to 1 hour at 325°. Brush top of crust with melted margarine or salt water solution, depending on taste. Makes one loaf.

LIMPA

This is a Swedish rye bread. A novel bread pan that makes an unusual round loaf is a clay flower pot dish (the part you set the pot in), lined with foil and oiled. The bread comes out round, and it tastes delicious because of the properties of the clay dish.

> 2 cups milk (sweet or sour)
> 1/3 cup dark molasses
> 1/4 cup melted shortening
> 1 package dry yeast
> 1/4 cup lukewarm water
> 2 cups unbleached white flour
> 2 teaspoons salt
> 2 cups rye flour
> 2 cups whole wheat flour
> 1/3 tablespoon caraway seed or grated peel of 1 large orange (optional)

Sift flours, then measure separately. Dissolve the yeast in 1/4 cup of warm water and let stand for 10 minutes. Add the yeast, salt, and molasses to the milk. Add the caraway seed or orange peel, if you are using it. Slowly beat in 1-3/4 cups of white flour. Add the shortening. Gradually stir in the rye and whole wheat flours to make a stiff dough. Sprinkle remaining 1/4 cup of flour on a breadboard and turn out the stiff dough onto the board; cover with the bowl and let stand for 10 minutes, then knead lightly for 10 minutes. Round dough into a ball and return to washed, greased bowl, turning once to bring greased side up. Cover and let rise in a warm place until double, about 1-1/2 hours. Turn dough onto lightly floured board, cut in half, round up portions, cover with bowls, and let stand 10 minutes. Shape into loaves, place in bread pans and let double in size again (about 1-1/2 hours). Bake for 1 to 1-1/2 hours, with middle-of-the-day sun. Cook one loaf at a time. When done, turn out of the pan at once to cool. Makes 2 round loaves.

CROWN COFFEECAKE

> 5 cups flour
> 2 packages dry yeast
> 1/4 cup warm water
> 3/4 cup milk
> 1/2 cup sugar
> 2 teaspoons salt
> 3/4 cup butter, melted
> 2 eggs, beaten
> 1/2 cup slivered almonds
> 2 teaspoons cinnamon

Dissolve yeast in warm water. Beat together 1-1/2 cups flour, yeast and water, warm milk, 1/2 cup sugar, salt, and margarine. Add beaten eggs and another cup of flour. Beat until the batter is smooth. Slowly add the rest of the flour until you have a light, smooth dough. Place in buttered bowl and brush with 1/2 cup melted butter. Cover, put in a warm place, and let rise until double in size. (This dough is very slow-rising.) Punch down and let stand 10 minutes. Combine cinnamon and 1 cup sugar. Sprinkle the bottom of a 10" tube pan with the almonds and 1-1/2 tablespoons of the sugar-cinnamon mixture. Pinch off pieces of dough and shape in balls 1-1/2" in diameter. Roll in the remaining 1/4 cup melted butter and then in the sugar mix. Place in the tube pan and let rise until double in size. Bake in a 325° oven for about an hour. Makes one large loaf.

SOURDOUGH PANCAKES

Sourdough pancakes are great made on the reflector cooker, and any leftover dough can be turned into a dough for light rolls.

> 1/2 cup sourdough starter
> 1 cup undiluted evaporated milk
> 1 cup warm water
> 1-3/4 - 2 cups flour
> 2 eggs
> 2 tablespoons sugar
> 1/2 teaspoon salt
> 1 teaspoon baking soda

Combine starter, milk, water, and flour in a large bowl; mix to blend and leave at room temperature overnight. Next morning add eggs, sugar, salt, and baking soda and mix well. Don't beat. Cook on a greased griddle over medium heat. Turn pancake when the top side is full of broken bubbles and has lost its glossiness. Makes 30 small pancakes.

SOURDOUGH HOT ROLLS

Leftover batter can be used for sourdough rolls. Simply add flour and salt. The proportion of flour to salt is one cup to 1/2 teaspoon salt. The amount you need depends on how much batter you have left. Just keep adding the flour mixture until the consistency is right.

> 1 recipe of Sourdough Pancakes
> 2 cups flour
> 1 teaspoon salt

Mix ingredients and turn out on a floured board. Knead, adding flour as necessary, until you have a smooth ball. Place in a greased bowl, brush with melted butter and let rise for about 1 hour. Punch down and knead again, adding flour if necessary. Roll out to about 3/4" thick. Cut with cutter, dip each roll on both sides in melted butter, and place rolls just touching in the pan. Cover and let rise until doubled (about 1 hour). Bake at 325° for 45 minutes. Makes 2 dozen rolls.

PIZZA

For best results plan to cook your pizza at noon when the oven is level and the sun directly overhead.

Dough
1/2 cup warm water
4 teaspoons vegetable oil
1/2 teaspoon salt
1 package dry yeast
1-1/2 cups flour

Combine water, 1 teaspoon vegetable oil, salt, and dry yeast. Don't stir. Let stand 5 minutes. Knead in flour and then 3 teaspoons of vegetable oil.

Sauce
8-ounce can tomato soup
1 clove garlic, minced
1/2 medium onion, grated
1/2 teaspoon Italian seasoning
1/4 teaspoon salt
3/4 cup shredded mozzarella cheese

Combine the ingredients, except the cheese, in a saucepan and simmer on the reflector cooker for 10 minutes or until slightly thick. Spread the dough in a 13" round pan. Spread sauce on top and sprinkle with cheese. Bake at 325° for 1/2 hour. Makes one 13" pizza. Other cheeses (cheddar or provolone), green peppers, mushrooms, or pepperoni can be added.

8

VEGETABLES

According to nutritionist Adele Davis in *Let's Cook It Right,* when vegetables are cooked with water, the vitamins are leached out and lost. Baking is far superior to boiling as a method of cooking vegetables. The solar oven lends itself beautifully to this nutritious and tasty way of preparing vegetables, legumes, and vegetable casserole dishes. The reflector cooker is used to saute, boil, or steam.

When baking in the solar oven, remember to warm up the oven first. Wash the vegetables and put them in a plastic oven bag, close with a twist, and place in the oven. For additional nutrition and flavor you can place the vegetables, plastic bag and all, in a brown grocery bag before inserting into the oven, and cook them in a covered casserole dish. The vegetables should cook as quickly as possible in the beginning. After they are warmed through, slow cooking is best so that they do not shrivel and become unattractive and tasteless. I wash my oven bags and reuse them as an economy measure. Do not use ordinary plastic bags for cooking—they aren't designed for that and could have toxins in them.

Do not add water or salt to the vegetables. You can add other spices for flavor, but salt will draw the vitamins from the vegetables, so try to add salt right before serving if it's needed. Cooking the vegetables whole takes longer, but the vitamins are more apt to escape from cut vegetabes. However, when the vegetable is cut, trimmed, or grated, add a little vegetable or olive oil to coat it and seal in the juices. This will prevent unnecessary loss of vitamin C. Do not use butter or margarine until just before serving; if cooked with the vegetables, the butter or margarine loses valuable vitamin A.

If you eat lots of vegetables, as we do, much of the time you will simply wash and clean the vegetables and cook them plain. We find that vegetables have so much more flavor when cooked in the solar oven that we enjoy them this way.

What I like to do is combine two or more vegetables, then add some onion slices, a clove of garlic, bell pepper pieces if I have some on hand, even chunks of fresh tomato—or any combination of these. We like to use a little olive oil with our vegetables; if used sparingly there isn't a strong taste of olive oil and yet there is a nice flavor and additional nutrition. I some-times put several kinds of squash together. If I want to give the dish an Italian flavor, I add a little basil or a combination of Italian seasonings.

Sometimes I grate a good cheese (one that's been aged at least six months), empty the vegetables into a serving dish, sprinkle with the cheese, and place the vegetables back in the oven for a few minutes to allow the cheese to melt. My family really loves vegetables this way. For added nutri-tion and flavor, you can sprinkle the vegetables with sesame or hulled sunflower seeds.

Because the vegetables are often somewhat cold when placed in a 350° oven, the temperature will drop to 325° or lower. It will take about 45 min-utes for vegetables like squash or cauliflower pieces to cook. If the vegetables are grated, cooking time is greatly reduced.

MAYONNAISE AND YOGURT SAUCE

I like to serve this as a vegetable topping.

1 cup mayonnaise
1 cup yogurt
2 tablespoons lemon juice or vinegar
1 teaspoon Worcestershire Sauce
1/2 teaspoon dry mustard
2 - 4 tablespoons grated onion
2 tablespoons finely chopped parsley
Dash cayenne

Combine ingredients in order listed. Blend well. Makes 2 cups.

SHREDDED BEETS

Shredded beets will be eaten by people who would ordinarily spurn this veg-etable.

4 - 6 medium beets
1 tablespoon lemon juice or 2 tablespoons vegetable oil
1/2 teaspoon salt
1 tablespoon butter or margarine

Wash beets thoroughly. Trim and shred, but do not peel. Toss with either the lemon juice or oil. Cook in the oven for 1/2 hour. Add salt and butter or margarine. Serve piping hot, but crisp. Serves 4.

GRATED CARROTS

> 6 carrots
> 1 cup fresh crushed pineapple
> 1/2 cup raisins
> Nutmeg
> Salt

Grate the carrots coarsely. Place in an oven bag or covered heated casserole dish with the pineapple and raisins; cook in a 300° - 325° oven about 20 - 30 minutes. Season with salt and a little nutmeg after removing from the oven. Serves 4.

SAUTEED ZUCCHINI

> 3 medium zucchinis, sliced
> 1/4 cup oil
> Juice of 1 lemon
> 1 garlic clove

Saute the squash in the hot oil, lemon juice, and garlic. Cook until nice and crisp. Some of the chips might be a little transparent, but serve the squash very crisp. Serves 4.

DILLED ZUCCHLNI

> 2 medium zucchinis
> 1/2 teaspoon dill weed
> 1 tablespoon melted butter

Cut 2 unpared medium zucchinis in half lengthwise. Place in oven and cook until tender, about 40 minutes. Brush with melted butter and sprinkle with dill weed. Makes 4 servings.

BAKED ZUCCHINI

> 2 zucchinis
> I tablespoon butter

Wash and slice zucchinis in round chips and cook in a plastic bag in your solar oven for at least 30 minutes for a semi-soft squash. Season with butter. Serves 4.

BUTTERNUT SQUASH

1 butternut squash
1/4 cup butter
1/2 cup brown sugar

Cut the squash in half and clean the fibrous insides and seeds from it. Place with the cut side down on a flat pan and cook in the solar oven for an hour or more at 275°. Then turn the squash over and sprinkle with the sugar and dot with the butter. Return to oven and cook another 15 minutes. Serves 2 - 4.

GREEN BEANS

2 lbs. green beans

Wash and string the beans. Cut the way you prefer, break into sections, or leave whole. Place in an oven bag and cook at 300° or more for at least an hour. The length of time depends on how crisp you like your vegetables. Serves 6 - 8.

POTATOES

My preference is to cook red potatoes in a plastic oven bag. If you prefer Irish potatoes, get your oven as hot as possible. They will cook more quickly if you insert a nail in each one. The more potatoes you cook, the more they will reduce the heat of the oven. Potatoes lower the heat more than meat does, so if you are having a crowd for dinner, consider settling for the smaller red potatoes that don't need as hot an oven.

ITALIAN FRIED LETTUCE

Use the outer leaves of iceberg lettuce (the ones you usually throw away) or romaine lettuce.

6 - 8 lettuce leaves
2 tablespoons olive or vegetable oil
1 clove garlic, minced
Salt
(2 slices beef bacon)
(leftover cooked vegetables)

If using the bacon, cut it into small pieces and brown well. Chop your leftover vegetables and brown them in the oil and garlic. Add the lettuce leaves and cook quickly, stirring constantly; the lettuce is done when it is transparent. Season with salt. Serves 4.

CORN

Husk, wash and trim fresh corn. Leave it on the cob and place in an oven bag. Cook for 20 minutes at 300° - 350°. It tastes just like steamed corn!

CORN PUDDING

8 - 10 medium ears of corn or 3 cups
1 teaspoon sugar
2 tablespoons flour
1/2 cup half & half
3 eggs
1 teaspoon salt
1/3 teaspoon pepper
3 teaspoons butter
Dash cayenne
Dash nutmeg

Scrape corn over large shredding surface of a food grater, letting kernels fall into a large bowl; also scrape each cob with back of a knife to remove pulp. Combine with sugar, flour, eggs, half & half, salt, pepper, cayenne, and nutmeg, stirring with a fork to blend well. Pour into an ungreased shallow 1 qt. casserole. Dot corn with butter. Bake, uncovered, in a 300° oven for 1 hour, or until pudding is set in the center when gently shaken. Spoon out to serve. Serves 4 - 6.

COLE SLAW

This is so easy to make, and yet so well-received!

3/4 cup vinegar
1/2 cup sugar
1-1/2 teaspoon salt
1 teaspoon dry mustard
1 cup salad oil
1 medium head of cabbage
2 - 3 green onions
(1 carrot, shredded)
(4 leaves red lettuce)

Combine first four ingredients in saucepan and bring to boil. Remove from heat and add 1 cup salad oil. Shred cabbage and green onions. If desired, add a little shredded carrot and red lettuce for color. Pour liquid over the cabbage, onions, and carrot mixture. Cover tightly. Refrigerate overnight. Serves 8 - 10.

BROCCOLI AND RICE

This is a good way to use the stems of your broccoli which you might otherwise discard. Be sure to peel them (the tough outer skin can be taken off very easily), cook them in a covered pan with a little water on top of the reflector cooker, then chop and combine with any leftover tops you might have.

> 1-1/2 cups of chopped broccoli cooked
> 2 cups cooked rice
> 1 cup sour cream
> 10-ounce can cream of chicken soup

Combine broccoli, rice, sour cream, undiluted chicken soup, salt, and pepper and place in an oiled casserole. Bake for 45 minutes to an hour until firm. Serves 4.

ARTICHOKE AND LIMA BEAN SUPREME

This is a most delightful vegetable combination. It's a little more expensive than the usual vegetable dish, but it's worth the price for a special occasion. It is so good that it can even be served cold, once cooked. The friend with whom this recipe originated likes to use fresh vegetables, but since they are hard to obtain in some areas, this recipe will include frozen vegetables. If you're cooking for a crowd, other vegetabes can be added, such as tiny baby peas and asparagus.

> 9-ounce package frozen baby artichokes
> 10-ounce package frozen baby lima beans
> 1 tablespoon olive oil
> 1 clove garlic, minced
> Bac-O-Bits

Combine the partially thawed vegetables in an oven bag. Add the oil and garlic and place in the solar oven at 300°. Cook until hot. After pouring into the serving dish, sprinkle with Bac-O-Bits. Serves 6.

STRING BEANS SUPREME

> 10-ounce package frozen string beans or I lb. fresh beans
> 1/2 cup chopped onion
> 1 cup sour cream
> 4 tablespoons margarine or butter
> 1 cup bread crumbs
> 1/2 cup grated cheddar cheese

If you are using fresh beans, cook them in a small amount of water on the reflector cooker or pre-cook them in the oven. Saute the chopped onion in 2 tablespoons of butter, add string beans and mix together with the sour cream. Brown the bread crumbs in 2 tablespoons melted margarine or butter, sprinkle over the string bean mixture, and top with the grated cheege. Bake in the solar oven until the cheese is melted and the other ingredients are hot, about 30 - 45 minutes. Serves 4 - 6.

AVOCADO SOUP

    3 cups chicken or vegetable broth
    1/4 cup chopped onions
    2 tablespoons vegetable oil
    2 small zucchinis, thinly sliced
    1 teaspoon seasoning salt
    1/4 cup lemon juice
    1 avocado, cut in large chunks

Saute the onion in the oil. Add the broth and bring to a boil. Add the zucchini, salt, and lemon juice and cook until the squash is barely tender. Just before serving, add the avocado. Serves 4.

9

LEGUMES AND GRAINS

Cooking time for dry beans, peas, and lentils is shortened when they are soaked before cooking. However, vitamins and minerals then pass into the water so vegetables should be cooked in the water used for soaking.

According to nutritionist Adele Davis, if soybeans are frozen after they have soaked and before they are cooked, cooking time is decreased by about 2 hours and they taste more like navy beans.

Sometimes I just let my beans soak in the refrigerator, thereby protecting the legumes from vitamin loss. A good rule of thumb is to use twice as much water as dry beans. In other words, if you put one cup of beans to soak, use two cups of water. I prefer to season my legumes with salt after they have been softened by cooking, although many recipes recommend putting the salt in from the start.

If the legumes are not soaked before cooking, they should be dropped quickly into boiling water so that the starch grains burst and water is absorbed rapidly. This shortens the cooking time. Heat should be lowered immediately to prevent the protein from becoming tough. Just turn the reflector cooker off focus. Just a word of caution here—remove your cooking pot from the reflector stove while you are making the new adjustment. After all, it isn't quite like a countertop stove, and you don't want beans all over the ground. A simmering temperature should then be maintained for the remainder of the cooking time. With a little practice and experience you will soon learn to adjust your reflector cooker so that you won't need to check on it more than once every hour or so.

Never put soda in your cooking water if you wish to maintain maximum vitamin B content. If salt, fat, or molasses are added at the beginning of cooking, the cooking time is prolonged. Add these ingredients after the legumes are tender.

Soybeans differ from other beans in that they contain about three times more protein, a small amount of sugar, and no starch. They supply essential amino acids, calcium, and B vitamins. Although relatively new to America they are now available as dried green soybeans which many have found to be more delicious than other varieties and cook in a somewhat shorter time.

LENTILS

These are to be cooked on the reflector cooker in a 1-1/2 quart saucepan.

> 2 tablespoons oil
> 1/2 onion, chopped
> 1 small clove garlic
> 1 cup lentils
> 2 cups water
> Salt and pepper

Saute the onion and garlic in the hot oil, add the lentils and brown slightly. Add the water and seasonings and cook at least an hour; longer is better. Serve over rice. Serves 4.

SPLIT PEAS

You can substitute lentils for the split peas. You can also omit any of the vegetables or add different ones.

> 2-1/2 cups meat stock or vegetable broth
> 1 cup dry split peas
> 1 onion, chopped
> (1/2 cup chopped tomatoes)
> (2 carrots, diced)
> (2 stalks celery with leaves, chopped)
> (1/4 cup grated cheese)
> 1 bay leaf
> 1/2 teaspoon thyme
> Salt and pepper
> Butter or margarine

Bring the stock to a full boil. Drop the dry split peas quickly into the boiling broth. Reduce the heat and simmer 30 minutes, or until the peas are tender. (Turn the reflector off focus to simmer). Add the onion, tomatoes, carrots, celery, seasonings, and butter or margarine. Cook until the vegetables are tender. Sprinkle with cheese before serving. Serves 4 - 6.

COOKED SOYBEANS

This recipe is for plain cooked beans. You can add seasonings and even jazz up the soybeans to taste like a delicious chili bean soup by adding tomato puree, a tablespoon of chili, and a teaspoon of cumin along with salt and pepper to taste.

> 1 cup dry soybeans
> 2 cups water or vegetable broth

Soak the beans in water overnight in the refrigerator, or if convenient, soak in an ice tray 2 hours or longer. Bring 2 cups of water or vegetable broth to boil over the reflector cooker and drop the soybeans into the water. The water will immediately return to a boil, so take the pot off the stove or turn the cooker so that it is slightly off focus. Replace the pot of beans, cover with a lid and let simmer covered for about four hours. Add water when needed. Serves 4.

ROASTED SOYBEANS

A really fun way to fix soybeans is to roast them in your solar oven. They can be seasoned so many different ways and are quite like nuts to eat. They can be used for snacks between meals or are nice as a party appetizer.

    1 cup dried soybeans
    2 cups water
    1/4 cup olive oil
    Salt or garlic salt

Soak beans in water overnight in the refrigerator. Next morning pour off the excess water and dry the beans with a paper towel. Spread the soybeans in a large flat pan and put in your solar oven at 200°. (This could be your cloudy day cooking.) Leave the beans for three hours, stirring occasionally. Then add olive oil and salt or garlic salt to taste and cook another 15 minutes. Store in an airtight container. If your roasted soybeans aren't dry enough, or if they collect moisture from the air, place them in the oven at 300° for another half hour. I like to add sunflower and/or sesame seeds to these beans. Sometimes I spice them up with a tablespoon of chili powder. Creative cooks can probably think of many other ways to garnish them. They are so delicious!

DRIED BEANS

    2 cups dried navy, lima, kidney or pinto beans
    1 quart water
    1 - 3 teaspoons salt
    1/2 teaspoon pepper
    3 - 4 tablespoons vegetable oil

Soak beans in water overnight in the refrigerator. Bring to a boil over the reflector cooker and simmer for 2 to 2-1/2 hours or until tender. Add water as needed. After the beans are tender, season with salt, black pepper, and vegetable oil. Serves 4.

OVEN RICE

I use a natural rice, so it takes longer to cook than processed rice. If you're cooking on a low-sun day, cook the rice longer than called for in the recipe.

    2 cups water
    1 cup rice
    1 teaspoon salt

Combine ingredients and place uncovered in 300° oven for one hour and 15 minutes. The rice is done when water is cooked away and rice looks dry.

HAPPY DAYS RICE

    1 cup rice
    2 cups boiling water
    2 teaspoons salt
    3 eggs
    1/2 cup butter, softened
    12-ounce can bean sprouts, drained
    1 cup chopped green onions, bottoms and tops
    1/3 cup pimentos
    Dash pepper

Before assembling the above ingredients, place a pan of water large enough to hold mold in the oven to start heating. Boil rice in 2 cups water and 1 teaspoon salt over the reflector cooker. When done, drain well. Whip eggs in butter and add to rice. Add bean sprouts, onions, pimentos, 1 teaspoon salt, and pepper. Mix well and pack into a well-greased mold. Set in pan of hot water and steam for about an hour and 15 minutes at 300°. It's done when a knife inserted into the mixture comes out clean.

BULGUR

This grain is exceptionally high in nutritional value and can be prepared much the same way as rice. So whenever rice is called for, for a new taste treat try this delicious wheat grain. It can be prepared either in the solar oven or on the reflector cooker. This recipe is to be used on the reflector cooker.

    1 cup bulgur
    2 cups cold water
    1/2 teaspoon salt

Place water in a small cooking pot, add salt and bulgur. Cover, bring to boil, reduce heat and simmer for 15 minutes. Serves 4 - 6.

HOPPING JOHN

    16-ounce package shelled blackeyed peas
    3 tablespoons vegetable oil
    1 cup finely chopped onion
    1 clove garlic, minced
    1 cup raw bulgur
    3 cups broth or water
    1-1/2 teaspoon salt

In a small frying pan, heat the oil and saute the onion and garlic. Set aside. Put water in a 1 qt. saucepan, place on the reflector plate, and bring to a boil. Drop the peas into the boiling water and add the salt; cook for 15 - 20 minutes. Then add the bulgur, onion, and garlic and cook slowly for another 15 minutes. Serves 6.

10

CASSEROLES

The nice thing about casseroles is that they are so convenient! You can prepare several of them at one time and freeze them. Here's one way that working women can use the solar oven. Take a frozen casserole from the freezer and put it in the oven before leaving for work with the oven focus at the noontime direction. The casserole defrosts, cooks, and stays warm until evening. I like to use a casserole for our evening meal in the summertime. I start cooking the casserole at 3:00 in the afternoon when the sun is still high enough to give me a good oven temperature, cook my casserole for the required time, and then let the sun move off focus to keep it warm until we eat at 5:30.

It's so easy to cook casseroles in the solar oven, because a constant temperature is not critical. Many times a casserole is much better when cooked slowly. Here is a meal you can cook later in the day, or on a day that is the sunniest.

MORE

This is a favorite recipe and one that our family has liked for years. We call it More simply because that's what you want after the first helping. You can make this for a crowd, or put it in a couple of family-size pans and freeze.

> 1/2 pound hamburger
> 1/2 pound sausage meat
> 1-pound can whole-kernel corn or three fresh ears of corn
> 2-ounce jar of pimentos
> 10-ounce can tomato soup
> 15-ounce can tomato sauce
> 6-ounce can olives, sliced in large pieces
> 2 large onions, chopped
> 1/2 pound fresh mushrooms, sliced
> 1 pound extra-wide noodles
> 2 cloves garlic, minced
> 1 large green pepper, chopped

1 tablespoon Worcestershire sauce
1 tablespoon chili powder
1/2 pound cheddar cheese, grated
Salt

Cook the noodles on the solar hot plate according to the directions on the package. Cook the meat along with the onions and drain off all the fat. Combine the rest of the ingredients, except the cheese, and add to the noodles. Pour into a very large casserole or two smaller casserole dishes. Cook until heated through, about 45 minutes. Top with cheese the last 15 minutes. Serves 8 - 10.

BROCCOLI AND RICE CASSEROLE

1 pound fresh broccoli, cooked and drained
2 cups cooked rice
10-ounce can cream of chicken soup
1 cup shredded cheddar cheese
12-ounce can water chestnuts, drained, or 1/2 cup slivered almonds
1/2 cup cracker crumbs
2 tablespoons butter, melted

Add the cheese to the hot cooked rice; stir well. Add broccoli, soup, and almonds or water chestnuts. Combine the cracker crumbs with the melted butter and sprinkle over top of casserole. Bake at 300° for an hour. Serves 4 - 6.

QUICHE LORRAINE

This is a favorite recipe of our daughter, Jessica. It's delicious and easy to make. Use the oil pastry recipe in the dessert section for the crust. Precook the crust for 30 minutes.

3/4 cup mayonnaise
2 tablespoons flour
2 eggs, beaten
8 ounces gruyere cheese, cubed
2 tablespoons Bac-O-Bits

Blend the flour into the mayonnaise. Add eggs and cheese. Pour into a 9" pie shell and sprinkle Bac-O-Bits on top. Bake at 300° - 325° for one hour. You can reheat this pie or even serve it cold. Serves 6.

Variations:
1/2 cup celery, chopped
1/2 cup scallions, chopped
6-ounce package crab meat, drained
6-ounce package shrimp, drained

Combine all or part of the above with the cheese mixture and pour into the pie shell.

CHILI RELLENOS BAKE

I call this my "rainy-day special" because I've baked it on some of our more overcast days. Ordinarily it would have been done in an hour, but since the oven temperature never got above 225°, I left it in for two hours. Is it ever delicious! This is one of my favorite casserole main dishes; it's even good the next day served cold.

    8 fresh-roasted, peeled, and seeded chili peppers
    6 ounces sharp cheddar cheese, shredded (1-1/2 cups)
    2 cups milk
    4 eggs, beaten
    1/4 cup flour
    1/2 teaspoon salt

    Layer the chilis in an 8" square casserole; sprinkle with cheese. Combine remaining ingredients and beat until smooth. Pour over chilis and cheese. The casserole is done when a knife inserted comes out clean. Serves 4 - 6.

CHILI BEEF CASSEROLE

Custard casseroles don't need much attention. They seem to be made for solar cooking. You can cook them until they're firm and leave them in the oven, off focus, to keep them warm.

    1/2 pound ground beef
    1/2 cup chopped onion
    1/2 teaspoon salt
    1/4 teaspoon pepper
    8 fresh-roasted, peeled, and seeded chilis
    1/2 cup shredded cheddar cheese
    1/4 cup flour
    1/2 teaspoon salt
    4 eggs, beaten
    1-1/2 cups milk

    Brown beef and onion in skillet; drain off fat. Sprinkle meat with salt and pepper. Place half the chilis in a 10" x 6" baking dish, sprinkle with cheese, and top with meat mixture. Arrange remaining chilis over meat. Mix flour and salt in bowl. Combine eggs and milk. Add egg mixture to flour gradually, beating until smooth. Pour over meat and chili mixture. Cook in 300° oven for about an hour. It's done when a knife inserted comes out clean. Let cool 5 to 10 minutes; cut in squares to serve. Serves 8.

ENCHILADA CASSEROLE

This casserole is made with turkey or chicken, so you can start from scratch or use leftover turkey.

    2 - 3 cups deboned chicken or turkey, cut in small pieces
    1 onion, chopped
    1 7-ounce can whole green chilis
    1 pint sour cream
    10-ounce can cream of chicken soup
    1 dozen corn tortillas
    1 cup shredded cheddar cheese

Tear the corn tortillas into bite-size pieces and place half of them on the bottom of greased 2-quart casserole. Add a layer of turkey or chicken and a layer of chopped onions and green chilis. Make another layer starting with the tortilla pieces. Mix together the sour cream and cream of chicken soup and pour over the top. Sprinkle with cheddar cheese. Bake for an hour at 300° or better, or until bubbly. Serves 6 - 8.

LASAGNA

    1 cup olive oil
    1/2 cup minced onion
    2 garlic cloves, crushed
    1 pound ground beef
    1/2 pound Italian sausage
    1 tablespoon sweet basil
    1 tablespoon salt
    1/2 teaspoon pepper
    12-ounce can tomatoes
    16-ounce can tomato paste
    3 tablespoons parsley
    1 pound lasagna noodles
    1 pound mazzarella cheese, shredded
    1 pound ricotta cheese
    2-1/2 ounces parmesan cheese

Brown beef, sausage, onion, and garlic in oil. Add seasonings, parsley, tomatoes, and tomato sauce; simmer 1/2 hour over reflector cooker. Cook lasagna as directed, drain, and rinse. Using a 2-quart casserole, alternate layers of lasagna, sauce, and cheese; end with sauce. Use Parmesan on top only. Bake at least one hour or until bubbly. Serves 8-10.

PEGGY'S EGGPLANT

Here's a nice recipe that can be used as a vegetable casserole, or you can add hamburger and use it as a main dish.

    3/4 cup garlic bread crumbs
    5 tablespoons butter
    1 clove garlic, minced
    1 medium eggplant, peeled
    2 medium bell peppers, coarsely chopped
    1/2 cup chopped onions
    1-1/2 teaspoon salt
    1/2 cup ricotta cheese
    3/4 cup milk

Melt 3 tablespoons butter, saute the garlic, onions, and bread crumbs in the butter. Cut the eggplant into 1" cubes. Combine the eggplant, green pepper, and seasonings with sauteed ingredients in casserole dish. Scald the milk and add 2 tablespoons butter; pour over the casserole mixture. Sprinkle the top with ricotta cheese. Bake at 300° for 55 minutes. Serves 4 - 6.

MANICOTTI

When preparing this dish, use the noodles in their uncooked form.

    Sauce
    2 tablespoons vegetable oil
    1/2 large onion, chopped
    2 cloves garlic, minced
    1/2 bell pepper, chopped
    3 chopped, peeled tomatoes
    1 15-ounce can tomato sauce
    1 tablespoon basil
    2 teaspoons salt

Saute the onion in the vegetable oil; add garlic, pepper, tomato tomato sauce, basil, and salt. Simmer until slightly thickened, about 15 - 30 minutes.

    Stuffing
    1 cup shredded mozzarella cheese
    1 cup creamed cottage cheese
    1/2 cup mayonnaise or 1 egg
    2 tablespoons basil
    1 teaspoon garlic salt
    12 manicotti noodles, uncooked
    1/4 cup parmesan cheese

Combine all ingredients except the Parmesan cheese; stuff noodles with the cheese mixture. Pour half of the sauce in the bottom of a 9" x 13" pan. Put the stuffed noodles on top of the sauce and cover with remaining sauce; sprinkle Parmesan cheese over sauce. Place the casserole dish in a large oven bag and cook 45 minutes in a 300° - 325° oven. Remove from the bag and return to the oven for 15 minutes. Serves 6 - 8.

GNOCCHI

3/4 cup corn meal
2 cups milk or water
1 egg
1 cup grated mozzarella cheese
1-1/2 teaspoon salt
Parmesan cheese
1/2 cup vegetable oil
2 cloves garlic
1/2 cup chopped onions
6-ounce can tomato paste
2-1/2 cups stewed tomatoes
1 teaspoon salt
1/4 teaspoon pepper

Put corn meal in saucepan and gradually add milk or water. Cook low heat over reflector cooker, stirring constantly until mixture thickens and comes to a boil. Boil 3 minutes. Remove from heat, add egg and beat well. Add the mozzarella cheese, salt and 1/4 cup of the oil. While still hot, pour into an 8" square pan. Let cool; then cut into 4" squares. Arrange the squares in a 9" x 13" pan with space between for the tomato sauce. Heat the remaining 1/4 cup of oil in a saucepan, add garlic, and cook for 8 minutes. Remove the garlic from the oil and add the onions, tomato paste, stewed tomatoes, salt, and pepper. After heating for a few minutes, pour sauce around the corn meal squares and sprinkle the top with Parmesan cheese. The yellow of the corn meal should show, so you have islands of yellow in the red tomato sauce. Bake at 300° for one hour. Serves 6.

CANNELONI

Stuffing
1 pound spinach
1 8-ounce package lasagna noodles
2 tablespoons melted butter
1 cup cottage cheese
1/4 teaspoon nutmeg
1/4 teaspoon basil
2 tablespoons parmesan cheese
2 eggs, beaten
1/2 teaspoon salt
Dash pepper

Cook the spinach in covered pan on reflector cooker. Doesn't need any water. Drain well; chop and cool. Cook the noodles and cut in half across the width. Combine the remaining ingredients with the chopped spinach; put one tablespoon of the mixture in the middle of each noodle and roll up. Place seam side down in casserole.

Sauce
1/4 cup butter
1/4 cup flour
1/2 teaspoon salt
1/4 teaspoon cayenne pepper
2 cups milk

Melt butter in a saucepan on the reflector cooker. Combine salt and pepper with flour; when the butter is bubbly add flour slowly, stirring constantly. Pour in millk; stir constantly until sauce thickens, about one minute. Pour sauce over stuffed noodles.

Topping
3 tablespoons crushed garlic croutons
3 tablespoons grated parmesan cheese
2 tablespoons melted butter

Sprinkle topping over sauce and noodles. Bake in hottest possible oven for about one hour. Serves 6.

11

POULTRY AND FISH

TURKEY

If you want to really amaze your friends, put a turkey in the oven as soon as you have any sun in the morning, attend church, then invite some friends home for dinner. When they see you take that nice, brown turkey from the oven they'll never stop exclaiming over the miracle of cooking with the sun!

If you let your oven warm up first to 350°, when you place your meat in the oven (your solar oven will take a bird 10 - 14 pounds), the temperature will drop 50° - 75°, and fluctuate between 275° - 325°. My first 12-pound turkey cooked in 3 hours, about 15 minutes per pound. This was a bit faster than I sometimes like to cook a turkey, but it's a guideline for you. If you want your turkey to cook more slowly, simply keep the oven a little off focus. If you want the turkey to cook while you're away, you can aim the oven to the position the sun will be in when you want the oven to "come on."

There are many variables, but remember that with poultry, you always want your oven temperature above 150° as protection against food poisoning. Any cook knows this, and there is no problem where solar cooking is concerned.

ROAST TURKEY BASTE

You can roast a turkey by simply placing it on a rack in a pan and possibly brushing with a little oil. If you'd rather, you can use an oven bag or even a large brown grocery bag. If you prefer your turkey basted, you might like to try something I learned years ago when I was a bride.

    1/4 cup flour
    1/4 cup margarine or butter, softened

Mix the margarine or butter with the flour and spread all over turkey. Bake.

TURKEY AND RICE JUBILLETTE

Rarely do we have a turkey that we don't have at least some left over. Here is one recipe that will keep turkey interesting for succeeding dinners.

    3 cups turkey, cubed
    3 tablespoons butter
    3 medium carrots, thinly sliced
    2-1/2 cups turkey or chicken broth
    1/4 teaspoon pepper
    1/2 teaspoon onion powder
    1/4 teaspoon powdered curry
    3 cups cooked white rice
    1/2 cup grated cheddar cheese

Saute carrots in butter until tender; add turkey, broth, and seasonings. Oil a 2-quart casserole dish and layer the rice and turkey in it. Pour any remaining broth over the top, then add cheese and bake about one hour at 300° - 325°. Serves 4 - 6.

DEE'S TURKEY TETRAZZINI

    3 - 4 cups turkey cut in 1" chunks
    2 tablespoons vegetable oil
    2 tablespoons flour
    1/2 teaspoon cayenne pepper
    6 cups turkey or chicken broth, or water
    1/2 pound mushrooms, sliced
    1 egg yolk, slightly beaten
    3 tablespoons light cream
    8-ounce package medium wide noodles
    2 tablespoons grated parmesan cheese
    1 teaspoon butter

Warm oil in the top of a double boiler; stir in flour, salt, cayenne, and one cup of the broth. Cook, stirring until thickened. Stir the egg yolk and cream slowly into the sauce. Add the turkey and mushrooms; heat thoroughly. Meanwhile, cook noodles in remaining broth 10 minutes or until tender. Arrange noodles in a shallow baking dish and pour on the turkey mixture. Sprinkle the top with Parmesan cheese and bake 45 ninutes in a 300° oven. It is done when bubbly. Serves 8.

TURKEY SOUP

There's no better way to achieve good nutrition than with soup. I have a good friend who says she never throws any food away. She saves vegetable peelings to be boiled for soup broth, leftover vegetables are either put in the blender or used whole in a soup. Above all, she never throws away the broth from the vegetables as it has a high vitamin and mineral content—and also makes delicious soup! Prepare in a 1-1/2 quart. saucepan.

3 cups turkey or chicken broth
1 cup turkey or chicken pieces
2 tablespoons brown rice
2 tablespoons chicken or turkey fat, or vegetable oil
1 small new potato, with the skin on
1/4 teaspoon sweet basil
1/4 cup chopped onions
1/4 teaspoon curry
1 teaspoon salt
pepper
1/4 cup orange juice
1 tablespoon white wine
1/2 orange, thinly sliced
2 tablespoons parmesan cheese

Brown the onion in the fat or oil until transparent. Liquefy the potato and broth in a blender and add to the onions. Bring both to a boil; add rice and cook until the rice is done. Add meat pieces and seasonings. Just before serving add the orange juice and wine. Float orange slices on top and sprinkle with Parmesan cheese. Serves 4 - 6.

TURKEY ALMONDINE

I cook this in my heavy pottery casserole. Start the pan warming in the oven before putting the casserole together, because the dish does hold the heat once warmed up.

2 cups cooked turkey, coarsely diced
4 tablespoons butter or margarine
4 tablespoons flour
1/2 cup chopped onion
2 cups milk
1-1/2 teaspoon salt
1 cup cooked peas
1/2 cup toasted slivered almonds
2 egg yolks
1/2 half cup bread or toasted corn flake crumbs
1 tablespoon butter
8-ounce package wide noodles
2 tablespoons parmesan cheese

Melt the butter and saute the onion until it is transparent. Add flour and blend in the milk. Stir until the sauce is smooth. Stir in the turkey, peas, and half the almonds. Beat the egg yolks with a fork; slowly stir 1/2 cup of sauce into the yolks until well mixed. Rapidly stir mixture back into the turkey sauce. Add to the noodles and pour into a 2-quart casserole. Scatter the crumbs and then the almonds on top; dot with butter. Sprinkle with Parmesan cheese. Bake in a 300° - 325° oven for one hour. Serves 8.

CHICKEN

The same rules apply to chicken as to turkey when cooking in your solar oven. The main difference is that your chicken will often be cut into pieces. However, when baking a chicken, follow the instructions in the turkey section for roast turkey.

Many people like to cook chicken with a "shake and bake," either their own combination of flour and spices or a commercial package. This works very well in the solar oven. Just coat the chicken with the shake and bake mixture, place it in a shallow baking dish, and let it cook in a preheated 350° oven. The temperature will drop a little when the meat is placed in the oven. Let it cook for approximately the same amount of time as it would cook in the kitchen oven.

CHICKEN BARBECUE

3-pound chicken, cut in pieces
1 medium onion, chopped
3 stalks celery, chopped
1/4 cup salad oil
2 cups stewed tomatoes
1 cup cider vinegar
1/4 cup lemon juice
6 tablespoons brown sugar, firmly packed
2 tablespoons prepared mustard
2 tablespoons Worcestershire sauce
1/2 tablespoon salt
1 tablespoons pepper

Saute onions and celery in the oil until translucent. Add tomatoes, vinegar, lemon juice, sugar, mustard, Worcestershire, salt, and pepper; simmer for 15 minutes, stirring occasionally. Dip chicken in the sauce and place in a shallow baking dish. Cook for 1-1/2 hours in a 275° - 300° oven. Serve with remaining sauce. Serves 6.

CORNISH HENS

4 Cornish hens
2 cups cooked wild or brown rice
1/2 cup finely chopped bell pepper
1/2 cup minced celery
1 cup minced onion
1 teaspoon salt
1 teaspoon basil
1 egg, slightly beaten
1/4 cup red wine
1/4 cup melted butter

Combine the rice, bell pepper, celery, and onion with the seasonings and wine. Stuff into the cavity of each of the Cornish hens. Brush with melted butter. Place in a flat pan and bake at 300° for 1-1/2 hours. Serves 4.

SPAGHETTI CHICKEN

This recipe for chicken is different and so good that our daughter Deirdre insisted that I place her endorsement on it. Some San Diego friends may recognize this recipe, too.

    3-pound broiler-fryer, cut in pieces
    3 tablespoons vegetable oil
    1/2 cup chopped onion
    1 clove garlic, minced
    2 cups tomatoes
    8-ounce can tomato sauce
    6-ounce can tomato paste
    2 tablespoons fresh parsley
    3 teaspoons basil
    1/4 teaspoon pepper
    8-ounce spaghetti cooked and drained
    Parmesan cheese

Heat the oil and cook onion and garlic until onion is transparent. Add remaining ingredients, except chicken, cheese, and noodles; mix well. Wash the chicken pieces and place in a shallow pan. Pour sauce over the chicken. Cook slowly for about 3 hours in a moderate oven. Remove the meat from the bones, place on noodles, and top with Parmesan cheese. Serves 6 - 8.

BESS' FABULOUS CHICKEN

An elegant company dinner; this recipe was given to us by a good friend.

    8 deboned chicken breasts
    8 slices of bacon
    2-1/2 ounces chipped beef
    10-ounce can cream of mushroom soup
    1/2 pint sour cream

Debone and skin the chicken breasts and cut in two. Wrap each chicken breast with a slice of bacon. Cover the bottom of a flat greased baking pan with chipped beef. Arrange chicken on the beef. Mix soup and sour cream and pour over the entire surface. Bake at 275° for about 3 hours, uncovered. Serves 8.

CHICKEN TERIYAKI

This has been a favorite recipe of ours through the years. Prepare and serve Chicken Teriyaki over or beside rice.

    2 or 2-1/2 pound chicken, cut in pieces
    1/2 cup Teriyaki sauce
    Grated fresh ginger root, to taste

Marinate the chicken in the sauce and ginger root for 4 hours, turning frequently. Remove the chicken from the sauce and bake in 275° - 325° oven for 1 hour. Serves 6.

FISH

Many people have told me they aren't fond of fish. Even my family gave me some static on this until I learned that strong "fishy" odors or taste can be minimized with the use of wine, vinegar, ginger, onions, or garlic. Baked fish recipes lend themselves very well to our tastes and I actually get rave reviews for these recipes. Fish takes very little heat to cook and is great to bake in a solar oven.

BAKED HADDOCK OR SOLE

    2 pound fish fillets
    1/4 cup butter or margarine
    1-1/2 cups bread crumbs
    1 cup grated Monterey Jack cheese
    1/4 cup sherry
    Salt
    Pepper

Wash the fish, pat dry with paper towels, and place in 8" square pan. Pour sherry over the fish, and add salt and pepper to taste. Saute the bread crumbs in the butter and sprinkle over the fish; sprinkle the cheese over crumbs. Bake in a 300° oven for approximately 45 minutes. The fish is done when it flakes with a fork. Serves 4.

BAKED RED SNAPPER

3 pounds red snapper or other large fish, whole
1 cup flour
Salt
Pepper
2 tablespoons butter
1/2 cup chopped onion
2 garlic cloves, chopped
8-ounce can tomato sauce
1 tablespoon Worcestershire sauce
1 tablespoon chili powder

Combine flour with salt and pepper to taste. Dredge the fish with the seasoned flour and place in a large flat pan. Saute onion and garlic until onion is transparent. Add tomato sauce, Worcestershire sauce, chili powder, salt, and pepper. Pour the sauce around the fish and bake in a 300° oven for one hour. Time will vary according to shape of the fish. A meat thermometer should read 140°. Serves 6.

FISH BAKED IN COVERED CASSEROLE

2 pounds fish, preferably in one large chunk
2 tablespoons butter, softened
1/4 teaspoon nutmeg
3 tablespoons sherry
3 tablespoons butter, melted
2 tablespoons capers
Chopped parsley
Salt

Have fish at room temperature. Combine 3 tablespoons butter, nutmeg, and sherry, and rub into fish on all surfaces. Place fish in a casserole with a close-fitting lid. Bake at 300° until tender. Do not overcook. Combine melted butter, capers, parsley, and salt. Pour over baked fish when removed from oven. Serves 4 - 6.

12

MEAT

The solar oven lends itself beautifully to cooking meat. The timing for cooking meat will be close to what it is in your inside oven. You could easily have more heat than you want in cooking your beef, because meat cooked at low temperatures tastes better and is more nutritious. Meats cooked slowly need little watching or work. When cooking meats two temperatures must kept in mind—the temperature inside the meat, and the external temperature. A meat thermometer is an inexpensive way to be sure about meat. Use it according to the directions.

When cooking roast beef, leg of lamb, or pork roast, remember that it draws the juices from the meat; so it's not advisable to season your meat before or during the roasting process. You really don't need to do anything to the meat, but you can brush a little oil on it to help seal in the juices. Interestingly, according to nutritionist Adele Davis, the old concept of sealing in the juices by searing the roast or steak is a fallacy. Instead, essential amino acids are broken apart by the heat and their health-promoting value is decreased.

You can pre-heat the oven, if you like. Something I have found works very well is to put the roast in the oven and then focus the oven ahead at the place where you want it to "come on." For example, if I left for church at 9:00 in the morning and wanted a 7-pound roast to be done when I got home at 12:30, I would aim the oven at the 10:30 sun position. If it was an overcast day and the roast wasn't quite done when I arrived home, I would just reposition the oven and cook the roast a while longer. Many times I put vegetables in with the roast, which helps keep the temperature lower. The more bulk you have in the oven, the more it pulls the temperature down. If you're late returning home, the sun usually moves off the oven, so the temperature gradually dropps. I won't say you can't burn the meat, but your chances are better that the roast won't burn in a solar oven.

In summer you can cook many of your evening meals in the solar oven. If you are cooking a roast or turkey, start by 3:00 in the afternoon, as the sun is quite low by 4:30 or 5:00 and your oven temperature begins to decrease. In winter do your solar cooking in the middle of the day.

If you're going to cook steak or hamburgers, your reflector cooker is the way to go. You have an instant 500° temperature with this cooker. One day in April at 4:30 in the afternoon, I set up the reflector cooker, placed

my frying pan on the grill and went inside to get three little filets. When I returned and put them in the pan, they sizzled immediately. They cook fast, too, so watch that you don't get them too well done. The grill isn't large enough to cook for a crowd, but three hamburger patties or three 1" thick filets work very well. To cook hot dogs, it's fun to use long forks and hold them over the grill.

SUN CHALUPA

This is a favorite recipe from daughter Jessica. She and her family live in the border town of El Paso, Texas, and use one of our ovens. All of us are great Mexican food fans.

    3 pounds chuck roast
    1 pound pinto beans
    6 or 7 cups of water
    1 chopped onion
    2 minced garlic
    1 tablespoon cumin
    2 tablespoons chili powder
    4-ounce can chopped green chilis

Clean and soak beans in water overnight. Combine with beef and seasonings and cook slowly for about 5 hours between 250° and 300° in covered porcelain roaster in solar oven. When the beef is very tender, break up and serve over flour tortillas or corn chips. Sprinkle grated cheese over the top. Serves 10.

SUN DOGS

    8 beef hot dogs
    2 1-pound cans barbecued beans
    1/2 cup catsup
    1/4 cup chopped bell pepper
    1/2 cup chopped onion
    1 teaspoon chili powder
    1/4 cup barbecue sauce
    8 ounces Monterey Jack cheese, shredded

Pour beans into baking dish. Combine catsup, bell pepper, onion, barbecue sauce, and chili powder. Slash hot dogs diagonally in several places. Place hot dogs on beans; cover with sauce. Top with shredded cheese. Bake for 45 minutes in a 275° oven. Serves 6 - 8.

SOLAR STEW

Here is a recipe given to me by one of my favorite neighbors. She said it was a favorite with them, and it proved to be just as well-received by my family.

    2 pounds stew meat
    1 package onion soup mix
    1/2 cup red wine
    10-ounce can cream of mushroom soup
    1/4 cup lemon juice
    1-pound bag frozen mixed vegetables

Combine all of the ingredients, except frozen vegetables, in a covered casserole. Bake slowly in a 250° oven for 3 hours. Or cook it all day at a lower temperature. Add a package of frozen mixed vegetables near the end of the cooking time. Serves 4.

SWISS STEAK AND VEGETABLES

    3 pounds round steak, 1-1/2" thick
    1/2 cup flour
    Salt
    Pepper
    1/4 cup vegetable oil
    6 whole new potatoes
    6-10 carrots
    1 onion, quartered
    2 cups water or vegetable broth

Season the meat with salt and pepper, coat it with the flour, and pound well with a meat pounder or the edge of a saucer. Cut into serving pieces and brown in hot oil on the reflector cooker. Remove from the oil when brown and place in a casserole dish or shallow pan. Cover with 2 cups of hot water or leftover vegetable broth. Put new potatoes, carrots, and onion on top of the meat. Bake in solar oven for 3-1/2 hours. Temperature can vary from 225° - 300°. Make gravy of juice left in the pan. Serves 6.

BEEF STRIPS ORIENTAL

    1 pound flank steak (partially frozen)
    4 tablespoons dry sherry
    4 tablespoons soy sauce
    5 tablespoons vegetable oil
    2 cloves garlic, crushed
    1 onion, quartered
    2 medium bell peppers, cut in wedges
    2 tomatoes, cut in wedges
    1 tablespoon cornstarch
    1 cup vegetable broth

The steak is partially frozen for easy slicing. Cut the meat into paper-thin strips, almost at right angles to the grain. Combine with the marinade of sherry, soy sauce, and 2 tablespoons vegetable oil. Set aside. Saute garlic in 3 tablespoons hot oil; discard the garlic. Add onion, bell pepper, tomatoes and heat until hot. Set aside. Cook the meat and marinade quickly, until meat is done. Dissolve cornstarch in vegetable broth, add to meat and cook until thickened and bubbly. Combine with the onion, peppers, tomatoes; serve over rice. Serves 4.

SWEET 'N SOUR MEAT LOAF

Meat Loaf
1-1/2 pounds ground meat
1/3 cup milk
2 eggs, beaten
1/2 cup minced onion
1 teaspoon celery salt
1/4 teaspoon pepper
1 tablespoon Worcestershire sauce
1 tablespoon prepared mustard
3 slices bread, crumbled

Combine milk, eggs, and seasonings. Add bread; crumble in beef and mix well. Shape into loaf and place in pan. Cover with Sweet 'N Sour sauce.

Sauce
1/2 cup chili sauce
2 tablespoons brown sugar
1 teaspoon prepared mustard
1 teaspoon horseradish

Mix ingredients well. Cover meat loaf with sauce and bake 1-1/2 hours at about 275°. Serves 4.

MEXICAN BEEF

This is a dish common to the southwest. It's usually called Beef Burros or Burritos.

Filling
4 pounds chuck roast
14-ounce can green chilis, diced
Taco sauce to taste
1 dozen medium flour tortillas
1 cup shredded cheddar cheese

After the roast is cooked in the solar oven for 2 or 3 hours at a low temperature (225° - 300°), it should be very tender. Drain off any excess fat and break the meat apart and shred with a fork. Next, mix with the green chilis and taco sauce. Put about 3 tablespoons of meat in the middle of a tortilla, fold the sides in and roll up neatly. Repeat this process with each tortilla and place in a shallow pan. Place in the solar oven and heat for 20 - 30 minutes.

Sauce

3 cups stewed tomatoes
1/2 onion, minced
1/2 bell pepper, diced
2 teaspoons chili powder
1/2 teaspoon cumin

Combine the ingredients and heat on the reflector cooker. Serve 2 burros to each person, topping with some of the sauce and sprinkled cheese. Serves 6.

SUNNY SOUTHERN POT ROAST

5 pounds pot roast
1/4 cup flour
1-1/2 teaspoons salt
1 teaspoon ginger
1/2 teaspoon allspice
1/4 teaspoon pepper
3 tablespoons bacon drippings
8-ounce can tomato sauce
1/2 cup cider uinegar
1/4 cup diced mushrooms
2 medium onions, sliced
2-1/2 tablespoons sugar
1 bay leaf

Mix flour and seasonings and coat the roast, rubbing in well. Brown well in bacon drippings. (It is easier to do this on the inside range.) Place in large pan. Pour on the remaining ingredients, first blending to combine flavors. Cook slowly in solar oven for at least 3-1/2 hours. Your temperature can vary from 250° - 325°. Serves 8.

BEST EVER BARBECUE BEEF

6 pounds chuck roast
3 large onions, chopped
2 stalks celery, chopped
2 large bell peppers, chopped
6 tablespoons barbecue sauce
20-ounce bottle catsup
1-1/2 cups water
3 tablespoons vinegar
Salt
Pepper

Cut up meat in small pieces and discard bone and fat. Combine the remaining ingredients. Put in a small porcelain roaster and cover with mix. Cook about 6 hours at 250°. Fork meat apart and take out fat. Refrigerate overnight and reheat to serve.

LAMB ROAST

Leg of lamb
1/2 cup flour
Garlic or lemon
Salt and pepper

Remove the roast from the refrigerator at least 1/2 hour before cooking. Pre-heat solar oven to 350°. Rub the lamb with garlic or lemon and dredge with flour. Place the lamb, fat side up, in a pan on a rack in the solar oven. Bake at 300° or less. At that temperature, the leg of lamb will require about 30 - 35 minutes per pound. Season with salt and pepper. Serve with mint jelly.

PORK CHOPS AU SOLEIL

4 pork chops
1/2 cup hot apple juice
1 tablespoon brown sugar
2 teaspoons or 2 cubes instant bouillon
1 tablespoon cooking oil
1/2 teaspoon caraway seed
1/2 small cabbage, cut in wedges
2 apples, cored, cut in wedges
1/4 cup finely chopped onion

Lightly brown chops in oil in frying pan. Put browned chops in square pan. Dissolve bouillon in hot apple juice. Combine with the remaining ingredients and pour over pork chops. Cook in a 300° or less oven until beautifully browned and bubbly. Serves 2 - 4.

FRUIT-STUFFED PORK LOIN

This is an exotic company dinner.

7 pounds pork loin roast
6-ounce package prunes, pitted
6-ounce package dried apricots
1 cup dark raisins
1 cup light raisins
2 cups water
1 cup brown sugar
1 bay leaf
Salt and pepper

Buy a loin of pork; have loin cut from the bone and flatten like a jelly roll. Salt and pepper to taste. Cook the dried fruit in the water; add the brown sugar and bay leaf to the fruit and cook until syrupy. Drain off the liquid and save. Lay the meat out flat and spread with the fruit. Roll up like a jelly roll and tie securely with string. Roast very slowly in a 250° oven. It will take about 35 minutes per pound. Use any extra fruit and syrup as a sauce to serve over individual portions of the roast. Serves 6.

BAKED HAM

1 7-pound ham
1 cup brown sugar
2 teaspoons dry mustard
1/4 cup pineapple juice
15-ounce can pineapple slices
1/4 cup whole cloves

Bake the ham on a rack uncovered in a 300° oven. Allow 30 - 35 minutes per pound. It is done when the meat thermometer registers 170°. An hour before the ham is done, remove and cover with a glaze. Mix together the brown sugar, mustard, and pineapple juice; spread the mixture over the ham. Pin the pineapple slices to the ham with toothpicks and dot with whole cloves. Return the ham to the solar oven to cook for another hour.

13

DESSERTS

Many people are surprised to see that the solar oven can actually bake cakes and pies. It was a real revelation to learn that I could cook many kinds of cakes at temperatures as low as 300°—everything from a fudge cake to an angel food cake. Of course there are times when the oven will be hotter than 300°, but it's nice to know that you don't need 350° and higher for desserts.

When baking cakes or pies you should cook them on the sunniest days, in the middle of the day if possible. I also recommend that the novice solar cook start with something simple like Apple Crisp or Blond Brownies and work up to the more difficult cakes and pies. Dark metal pans work best for me but you can use Pyrex if you prefer.

I'll admit that when I first started cooking desserts in the solar oven I had misgivings, but now it's become as easy as pie.

Happy solar baking. Don't let it go to waist!

PEARS CONTINENTAL

> 4 large pears
> 1/4 cup toasted almonds, chopped
> 1 tablespoon butter, melted
> 2 drops almond extract
> 3/4 cup sherry

Halve and core pears. Mix together the almonds, butter, and almond extract; put filling in the pear cavities. Put the pear halves in a baking dish, pour the sherry over them, and bake at 300° for 45 minutes. Serve hot or cold. Serves 4.

PEAR CRISP

My family likes to use fruit as a dessert. And this is one of our favorites because it's so easy.

6 pears
1/2 cup flour
1/2 cup brown sugar
1/4 cup butter or margarine
1 cup chopped nuts

Core the pears, leaving the skin on; cut each pear into eighths. Place in an 8" square pan. Blend the remaining ingredients, except nuts, with your fingers and sprinkle over the pears. Top with nuts and bake 45 minutes in a 300° oven. Serve hot or cold; top with whipped cream or Kahlua. Serves 6.

APPLE CRISP

3 cups sliced apples
1-1/4 cups raw brown sugar
1-1/2 tablespoons flour
Pinch salt
Pinch cinnamon
1/4 teaspoon baking soda
1/4 teaspoon baking powder
3/4 cup flour
3/4 cup oatmeal
1/2 cup margarine

Peel and slice the apples. Combine slices, 1/2 cup sugar, 1-1/2 table-spoons flour, salt, and cinnamon; place in a 2-quart casserole. Mix remaining ingredients with your fingers until blended. Spread over apples. Bake about 1 hour in 300° oven or until the top is crusty. Serves 6.

STRAWBERRY SAND TARTS

1 cup butter
1/2 cup powdered sugar
2-1/2 cups flour
2 teaspoons vanilla
3/4 cup finely chopped pecans
1 cup strawberry jam
1 teaspoon chili powder
1/4 cup barbecue sauce
8 ounces Monterey Jack cheese, shredded

Blend the butter, flour, vanilla, and pecans together; make the dough into little balls and place on sheet pan. Make a hole in each cookie with your thumb. Put strawberry jam, or any jam that has a nice, bright color, in hole and bake for 20 - 30 minutes at 300°. After removing tarts from the oven dust with powdered sugar by setting them in the sugar while they are still warm. Makes 4 dozen cookies.

SESAME SEED COOKIES

You can toast the sesame seeds by placing them in a frying pan on the reflector cooker. Do not add oil. Stir seeds constantly until brown.

1 cup sesame seeds, lightly toasted
1 cup flaked coconut
3/4 cup margarine or butter, softened
1 cup natural brown sugar
1 egg
1 teaspoon vanilla
2 cups unbleached white flour
1 teaspoon baking powder
1/2 teaspoon baking soda
1/2 teaspoon salt

Beat together the margarine or butter, brown sugar, egg, and vanilla. Sift together the flour, baking powder, baking soda, and salt; add the sifted ingredients to the butter mixture. Stir in the sesame seeds and coconut. Drop by the teaspoonful onto ungreased cookie sheet and flatten with fork. Bake in a 325° oven for 20 - 30 minutes. Makes 4 dozen cookies.

BETTY'S MOLASSES SUGAR COOKIES

3/4 cup shortening
1 cup sugar
1/4 cup molasses
1 egg
2 cups flour
1/2 teaspoon ground cloves
1/2 teaspoon ground ginger
1 teaspoon cinnamon
1/2 teaspoon salt
2 teaspoons baking soda

Melt shortening in a 3 - 4 quart saucepan over low heat. Remove from heat; let cool. Add sugar, egg, and molasses; beat well. Sift together flour, baking soda, cloves, ginger, cinnamon, and salt; add to first mixture. Mix well; chill. Form in 1" balls, roll in granulated sugar, and place on greased cookie sheet 2" apart. Flatten with a fork. Bake 15 - 20 minutes at 300° or better. Makes 4 dozen cookies.

BISCOTTI

This is an unusual Italian cookie that is not real sweet. It is crisp, munchy, and very habit-forming.

1/2 cup peanut oil
1/2 cup sugar
2 eggs
1-1/2 cups flour

1 cup slivered almonds
1 teaspoon anise extract

Blend the peanut oil, sugar, and eggs with a mixer for five minutes. Add the flour. Finally, add the almonds and anise extract. The dough will be quite sticky. Spread it out very thin in a 10" x 14" cake pan. Bake for about 30 minutes at 300°; take from the oven and cut on the diagonal for a diamond shape. Return to the oven and leave until the cookies are brown and quite dry. Makes 6 dozen cookies.

BLOND BROWNIES

My daughters have always liked to make this recipe because you mix everything up in the saucepan you melt the butter in!

1/4 cup butter or margarine
1 cup light brown sugar
1 egg, beaten
3/4 cup sifted flour
1 teaspoon baking powder
1 teaspoon vanilla
1/2 cup chopped nuts

Melt butter or margarine. Add sugar and let cool. Add egg to the cooled mixture. Beat in the remaining ingredients. Spread in a well-oiled 8" square pan. Bake for 45 min at 300°; cut in diamonds or squares. Makes one dozen brownies.

CORALEE'S DATE SQUARES

1/2 cup butter, softened
1/4 cup sugar
1-1/3 cups flour
2 eggs
1/2 teaspoon baking powder
2/3 cup chopped dates
1/2 teaspoon vanilla

Cream butter and sugar; stir in 1 cup flour until crumbly. Press into oiled 8" square pan. Bake for 35 minutes at 300° or until lightly browned. Meanwhile, beat brown sugar and eggs at medium speed until blended. Beat in the remaining 1/3 cup of flour and baking powder; add the dates and vanilla last. Spread over the baked layer and bake another half hour until golden brown. Cool. Makes one dozen squares.

COCONUT PECAN SQUARES

Dough
1/2 cup butter
1/2 cup dark brown sugar
1 cup flour

Mix ingredients well and press into 8" square pan, spreading batter evenly into the corners. Bake in 325° oven for 30 - 40 minutes or until brown.

Filling
1 egg
1 cup light brown sugar
1 cup coarsely chopped pecans
1/2 cup shredded coconut
2 tablespoons flour
1 teaspoon vanilla
Pinch salt

Beat egg until frothy. Gradually add sugar and beat until thick. Add remaining ingredients and mix well; spread over baked crust. Bake 30 - 40 minutes in a 325° oven until brown. Sprinkle with confectioners' sugar when cool; cut into 1" squares. Makes one dozen squares.

SUNNY LEMON CAKE

White or yellow cake mix
4 eggs
3/4 cup water
3/4 cup salad oil
1 package lemon Jello
1-1/2 cups confectioners 'sugar
1/4 cup lemon juice

Mix first five ingredients together and beat four minutes with electric beater. Bake in a 9" x 13" pan at 300° for 1 hour. Combine the confectioners' sugar and lemon juice to make the icing. Prick cake all over with a fork and pour the mixture over hot cake; return to the oven for a few minutes to set icing. Serves 16.

CARROT CAKE

Here's a cake that's good anytime, but it's especially good during the Christmas holiday season. It's also fun to cook in interesting shapes and sizes and to use as a gift.

Cake
2 cups sugar
3 cups sifted flour
2 teaspoons baking powder
1 teaspoon salt
2 teaspoons baking soda

2 teaspoons cinnamon
3/4 cup finely chopped nuts
3/4 cup vegetable oil
4 eggs
2 cups finely grated carrots

Beat eggs; add oil and grated carrots. Set aside. Combine sugar, flour, baking powder, salt, baking soda, and cinnamon. Add nuts, mixing well. Add eggs, oil, and carrot mixture. Pour into greased and floured bundt pan or two loaf pans. Bake in 325° oven for 1 hour and 15 minutes. It will cook beautifully at a lower temperature just adjust baking time.

Icing
6 tablespoons margarine
1 box No. 4 confectioners' sugar, sifted
8-ounce package cream cheese
2 teaspoons vanilla

Melt butter and let cool. Cream sugar and cream cheese with the electric mixer. Add vanilla and butter; beat until smooth. Put cake in refrigerator after icing, the icing is quite soft and inclined to run. Serves 15.

APPLESAUCE CAKE

The thing that makes this cake really good is homemade applesauce. Just cook your apples; when they are tender, mash them with a fork. Leave them a little chunky.

1/4 cup shortening
1/2 cup sugar
1/2 cup hot water
1 cup applesauce
1-1/4 cups flour
1 teaspoon baking soda
1 teaspoon cinnamon
1 teaspoon cloves
1/2 teaspoon nutmeg
1/2 teaspoon salt
1 cup raisins
1 cup nuts

Cream shortening and sugar. Add remaining ingredients and mix well. Bake in an 8" square greased pan at 325° for 45 minutes. The cake is done when it cooks away from the sides of the pan and the top springs back when you touch it. Serves 8.

SPEEDY SOLAR CHOCOLATE CAKE

This cake can be mixed in the pan you're going to cook it in.

    1-1/2 cups sifted flour
    3 tablespoons cocoa
    1 teaspoon baking soda
    1 cup sugar
    1/2 teaspoon salt
    5 tablespoons cooking oil
    1 tablespoon vinegar
    1 teaspoon vanilla
    1 cup cold water

Put your sifted flour back in the sifter; add the cocoa, baking powder, sugar, and salt. Sift the ingredients into an oiled 9" square pan. Make three grooves, or holes, in the dry mixture. Into one, pour the oil; into the next, the vinegar; into the next, the vanilla. Pour the cold water over it all. Mix until it's smooth and you can't see the flour. Bake at 300° for 45 minutes Serves 6.

ZUCCHINI CAKE

Cake
    1 cup cooked zucchini
    1-1/2 cups sugar
    3/4 cup cooking oil
    2 eggs
    1-1/2 cups flour
    1 teaspoon baking powder
    1 teaspoon cinnamon
    1/2 teaspoon baking soda
    1/4 teaspoon salt

Combine the first four ingredients and beat for two minutes. Sift the remaining ingredients together. Combine the two mixtures; pour into an oiled loaf pan. Bake at 300° for 1 hour, or until an inserted toothpick comes out clean.

Icing
    3-ounce package cream cheese
    1-1/4 cups powdered sugar
    2 tablespoons margarine
    1 teaspoon vanilla

Cream the first three ingredients; add vanilla. Spread on cooled cake. Serves 8.

BLACK BOTTOM CUPCAKES

These are among the yummiest cupcakes I've ever tasted. They're good whether you put sugar and nuts on the top or not. My daughter likes to use these cupcakes for children's parties because they don't need a messy frosting.

    8-ounce package cream cheese
    Dash salt
    1 egg
    1-2/3 cups sugar
    6 ounces chocolate chips
    1-1/2 cups flour
    1/4 cup cocoa
    1/2 teaspoon salt
    1/3 cup oil
    1 teaspoon baking soda
    1 cup water
    1 tablespoon vinegar
    1 teaspoon vanilla
    1/2 cup finely chopped nuts

Combine cream cheese, 1/3 cup sugar, and chocolate chips, and set aside. Combine 1/3 cup sugar and nuts in a second small bowl. Put the rest of the ingredients in a third bowl and mix well. Line a cupcake tin with paper baking cups; fill 1/3 full with cake mixture from the third bowl. Add a large tablespoon of the cheese filling and chocolate chips from the first bowl and sprinkle with the sugar and nuts mixture. Bake for 45 minutes in a 300° oven, or until a toothpick inserted in cakes comes out clean. Makes one dozen cupcakes.

APRICOT CHEWIES

This is my favorite cookie recipe because it is so easy, tasty (company good), and nutritious .

    6 ounces dried apricots
    3 cups shredded coconut
    14-ounce can sweetened condensed milk

Put apricots through the meat grinder on coarse or chop well. Mix all the ingredients together and drop from a teaspoon onto a buttered cookie sheet. Bake at 300° for 25 minutes or until toasty on top. Remove at once to a cooling rack. Makes 5 dozen cookies.

OIL PASTRY

When baking a pie that calls for an uncooked pie shell, I give it a running start in the solar oven for about 20 minutes at 300° or better.

    2 cups flour
    1/2 teaspoon salt
    1/2 cup salad oil
    5 tablespoons cold water

Sift together flour and salt. Pour salad oil and cold water into measuring cup. Do not stir. Add all at once to the flour mixture and stir lightly a fork. Form into two balls; flatten dough slightly. Roll each ball between two 12" squares of waxed paper. (Dampen table slightly so paper won't slip). Peel off top sheet of waxed paper and fit dough into pie plate. Makes two 9" crusts.

GRAHAM CRACKER PIE CRUST

    1-2/3 cup graham cracker crumbs
    1/4 cup sugar
    1/4 cup butter or margarine, softened

Combine the ingredients. Blend well with fingers, fork, or pastry blender. Pour crumb mixture into a 9" pie pan. Put an 8" pie pan on the crumbs and press firmly so that crumbs are molded to 9" pan. Remove 8" pan. Bake for 10 minutes; remove to wire rack to cool. Makes one 9" pie crust.

PECAN PIE

    3 eggs
    2/3 cup sugar
    1 cup light corn syrup
    1/4 teaspoon salt
    1/2 cup melted butter
    1/4 teaspoon vanilla
    1 cup pecan halves

Beat eggs slightly; add sugar, corn syrup, salt, butter, and vanilla. Mix thoroughly. Stir in pecan halves. Pour into a 9" pastry lined pie plate. Bake in a 300° oven for 1 hour and 15 minutes, or until set and pastry nicely browned. Makes one 9" pie.

CHOCOLATE SHOO FLY PIE

This pie is so delicious and so very easy to make.

    9" pie crust
    1/2 cup molasses
    1/2 cup boiling water
    2 tablespoons cocoa
    1/2 teaspoon baking soda
    1/2 teaspoon cinnamon
    1/2 teaspoon cloves
    1/2 cup flour
    1/2 cup sugar
    1/4 cup butter, softened

Bake the pie crust in the oven for 30 minutes. Combine the molasses, water, cocoa, baking soda, cinnamon, and cloves; let stand while preparing topping. Combine flour, sugar, and butter. Pour the molasses mixture into pie shell, top with crumb mixture, and bake 40 minutes in a 300° - 325° oven. Makes one 9" pie.

CHEESE PIE

Years ago a friend shared this recipe with me, and it's been an all-time favorite with our family and everyone we've shared it with. Use a graham cracker crust.

    Filling
    12 ounces cream cheese
    3/4 cup sugar
    2 eggs, beaten
    1 teaspoon vanilla
    2 teaspoons lemon juice

Allow the cream cheese to soften and then beat in the other ingredients. Pour into a graham cracker pie shell and bake at 300° for 25 minutes. Cool for five minutes.

    Topping
    1 cup sour cream
    1 teaspoon vanilla
    1 teaspoon lemon juice
    3-1/2 tablespoons sugar

Combine ingredients and spread over the top of the cooled cream cheese pie. Bake for 15 minutes at 300°. Refrigerate. Leave the pie in the refrigerator for several hours before cutting. Serves 6.

APPLE SCOTCH PIE

This is delicious made in either a graham cracker pie shell or a pastry shell. If you use the oil pastry, cook it in the solar oven at 300° for 15 - 20 minutes before filling with apples. This is good with cherries too. It can also be used without the pie crust and topped with whipped cream.

Filling
6 medium apples
    or 2 1-pound 4-ounce cans unsweetened apple pie filling
2/3 cup brown sugar, firmly packed
2 tablespoons flour
2 tablespoons lemon juice
Pinch salt
1 9" pie shell

Peel and slice the apples. Combine in a large bowl with the ingredients. Mix well and pour into the 9" pie shell.

Topping
2/3 cup flour
1/2 cup quick-cooking rolled oats
1/2 cup chopped nuts
1/4 cup sugar
1/2 teaspoon salt
1 teaspoon cinnamon
4-ounce package butterscotch pudding (do not use instant pudding)
1/2 cup butter, melted

Combine the ingredients in a large bowl and mix with fingers until crumbly. Sprinkle over the apples and bake in a 300° oven for one hour. Makes one 9" pie.

THE MINIMUM SOLAR BOX COOKER

A DESIGN YOU CAN BUILD IN 2-4 HOURS FOR ALMOST NOTHING

This past summer, experiments in Seattle and Arizona have proven that solar box cookers can be built more simply than even the simple method we have been using. Recent discoveries have paved the way for a simpler construction method that allows a cooker to be built in a few hours for very little money or resources. This might also be a good design to use in workshops, since less time would be spent on construction and more on a discussion of important solar box concepts, such as alternative materials, cooking methods, cultural issues, etc. The following developments make this design possible:

1. Insulation is not essential in the walls — a foiled airspace is all that is necessary.

2. Aluminum foil can be reduced to just one layer (though a layer on the inside of each box makes a hotter oven).

3. The airspace between the walls can be very small. The smallest airspace we've tested is one inch, but we suspect that even less would work.

4. Almost any size oven will cook. In general, larger ovens get hotter. But the limiting factor is still the ratio between the mass of the food and the size of the oven (we cooked a liter of beets in late-September in Seattle using an oven with an opening only 10" x 14" (25cm x 35cm).

5. Our experience shows that a double layer of plastic film works at least as well as a single sheet of glass.

6. Shallower ovens cook better since they have less wall area through which to lose heat. It's best for the inside of the oven to be just slightly taller than the biggest pot you plan to use.

A NEW SIMPLER DESIGN

Taking these factors into account, we are able to take our best shot at describing the minimum solar box cooker—one that can be built by anyone with access to cardboard, foil, glue (wheat paste works great), and plastic or glass.

WHAT YOU WILL NEED

Two cardboard boxes, homemade, scavenged, or bought. Almost any size will work. The proportion between the two boxes is not critical. We would suggest that you use an inner box that is at least 15" x 15" (38cm x 38cm). The outer box should be larger all around, but it doesn't matter how much bigger as long as there is an inch (2.5cm) or more of an airspace between the two boxes. Also note that the distance between the two boxes does not have to be equal all the way around. Thus, with rectangular boxes, the long sides might have a bigger airspace than the short sides or visa versa.

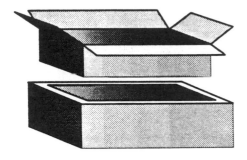

Figure 1

One sheet of cardboard to make the lid. This piece must be at least 3" (7.5cm) larger all the way around than the top of the finished cooker.

One small roll of aluminum foil.

One small jar of black tempera paint, or black soot from clear wood.

At least 8 ounces of white glue or wheat paste.

One Reynolds® Oven Cooking Bag (or sheet of glass). These are available in almost all supermarkets in the U.S. They are rated for 400° F (204.4 C) so they are perfect for solar cooking. They are not UV resistant; thus they will become more brittle and opaque over time and may need to be replaced periodically. (Barbara Kerr has experimented with the kitchen grade plastic wraps. Glad Wrap® is the only kitchen grade plastic film recommended at this time due to the chemical composition of all others investigated so far. Although it is not rated for the temperatures produced in solar ovens, it seems to work as glazing as long as the opening is not wider than the plastic. If the opening is wider than the plastic, sometimes the inherent cling will join two pieces. Some of these plastics, such as Saran Wrap® and the Reynolds Wraps® are made of Polyvinyline Chloride and there are still questions about their safety around food at solar box cooker temperatures).

CONSTRUCTION

BUILDING THE BASE

Fold the top flaps closed on the outer box and set the inner box on top and trace a line around it onto the top of the outer box, Remove the inner box and cut along this line to form a hole in the top of the outer box (Figure 1).

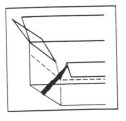

Figure 2

Decide how deep you want your oven to be (about 1" or 2.5cm bigger than your largest pot and at least 1" shorter than the outer box) and slit the corners of the inner box down to that height. Fold each side down forming extended flaps (Figure 2). Folding is smoother if you first draw a firm line from the end of one cut to the other where the folds are to go.

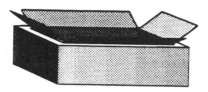

Figure 3

Glue foil to the inside of both boxes and also to the inside of the remaining top flaps of the outer box. Don't waste your time being neat on the outer box, since it will never be seen, nor will it experience any wear. The inner box will be visible even after assembly, so if it matters to you, you might want to take more time here. Glue the top flaps closed on the outer box.

Place some wads of crumpled newspaper into the outer box so that when you set the inner box down inside the hole in the outer box, the flaps on the inner box just touch the top of the outer box (Figure 3). Glue these flaps onto the top of the outer box. Trim the excess flap length to be even with the perimeter of the outer box. The base is now finished.

BUILDING THE LID

Take the large sheet of cardboard and lay it on top of the base. Trace its outline and then cut and fold down the edges to form a lip of about 3" (7.5cm). Fold the corners around and glue (Figure 4). Orient the corrugations so that they go from left to right as you face the oven so that later the prop may be inserted into the corrugations (Figure 6). One trick you can use to make the lid fit well is to lay the pencil or pen against the side of the box when marking (Figure 5).

To make the reflector flap, draw a line on the lid, forming a rectangle the same size as the oven opening. Cut around three sides and fold the resulting flap up forming the reflector (Figure 6), and appy foil to the flap on the inside.

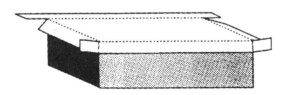

Figure 4

To make a prop bend a 12" (30cm) piece of hanger wire as indicated in Figure 6. This can then be inserted into the corrugations as shown.

Next, turn the lid upside-down and glue the oven bag (or other glazing material) in place. We have had great success using the turkey size oven bag (19" x 23 1/2", 47.5cm x 58.5cm) applied as is, i.e. without opening it up. This makes a double layer of plastic. The two layers tend to separate from each other to form an airspace as the oven cooks. When using this method, it is important to also glue the bag closed on its open end. This stops water vapor from entering the bag and condensing. Alternately you can cut any size oven bag open to form a flat sheet large enough to cover the oven opening.

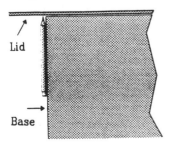

Lid

Base

Figure 5

Finally, to make the drip pan, cut a piece of cardboard, the same size as the bottom of the interior of the oven and apply foil to one side. Paint this foiled side black and allow it to dry. Put this in the oven (black side up) and place your pots on it when cooking.

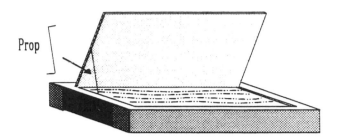

Prop

Figure 6

IMPROVING EFFICIENCY

The oven you have built should cook fine during most of the solar season. If you would like to improve the efficiency to be able to cook on more marginal days, you can modify your oven in any or all of the following ways:

1. Make pieces of foiled cardboard the same size as the oven sides and place these in the wall spaces.

2. Make a new reflector the size of the entire lid.

3. Make the drip pan using aluminum flashing and elevate this off the bottom of the oven slightly with small cardboard strips.

Courtesy of:

SOLAR BOX COOKERS NORTHWEST
7036 18TH AVE. NE
SEATTLE, WA 98115 USA
206-525-1418

COMMERCIAL SOLAR COOKING EQUIPMENT

Write to these firms for catalogs.

BURNS-MILWAUKEE INC.
4010 West Douglas Avenue
Milwaukee, Wisconsin 53209

Global Model SUN OVEN
Bantam Camper SUN OVEN

CLEVLAB
Box 2647
Littleton, Colorado 80181

Sunspot Backpacker
Astroven Camper
Helioven
Solarange

FISCHER SUN COOKER INC.
2797 Medford Avenue
Redwood City, California 94061

Fischer Sun Cooker Ovens (Oven and Parabolic Reflector)

SYNCRONOS DESIGN INCORPORATED
P.O. Box 10657
Albuquerque, New Mexico 87184

Solar Chef Solar Ovens
Ovenware

SOLAR BOX COOKERS INTERNATIONAL
1724 Eleventh Street
Sacramento, California 95814

Solar Box Cooker Plans
Completed Solar Box Cookers

Eleanor's Solar Cookbook
Cemese Publishers
7028 Leesburg Place
Stockton, CA 95207

BASIC SOLAR
7036 18TH Ave. N.E.
Seattle, WA 98115

Completed Solar Box Cookers

ABOUT THE AUTHORS

BETH HALACY

Beth has long been interested in solar energy applications; especially solar cooking. She greatly improved the solar cooker Dan first put together; suggesting more reflector area, double-glazing in a commercial model, and methods of better orienting the oven for higher temperatures. It was important to Beth to have an efficient, portable oven large enough to hold a 12" by 14" pan and enable solar cooks to prepare a proper meal. She formed a solar oven company in Glendale, Arizona, and managed the development, production, and marketing of high-performance factory-built solar ovens.

Already an excellent cook in the kitchen Beth developed or oven-tested all the recipes in *Cooking with the Sun* and has demonstrated them and the solar cookers in many places in addition to the Halacy homes in Arizona and Colorado. The original publisher of the book arranged an extensive personal appearance radio/TV solar cooking tour for Beth and daughter Deirdre in California — all the way from San Diego to San Francisco — and then sent Beth on to the Dinah Shore TV Show on location in Florida! Beth also organized and participated in a turkey-cooking demonstration in Illinois featuring 20 of her solar ovens built by local solar enthusiasts.

In Colorado, Beth recently hosted a solar cookout in a nearby park for a group of Boy Scouts, teaching them how to cook scrambled eggs and hot dogs on the solar reflector stove and bake cookies in the solar oven. This event was was a feature story in *Boys' Life magazine*

DAN HALACY

Dan attended the First World Symposium on Solar Energy in Phoenix, Arizona in 1955. In 1956 he joined the Association for Applied Solar Bnergy (which later became the *International Solar Energy Society*) and he began to design solar ovens and reflector cookers, as well as solar water heaters, solar stills, and even a solar-powered model airplane using lightweight photovoltaic cells. He holds two solar energy patents. His first solar energy book, *Fabulous Fireball*,was published in 1957 by Macmillan. In 1978, Beth and he co-authored *The Solar Cookery Book; Everything Under the Sun*, on which this revised edition is based.

Dan has been closely involved in solar energy for more than three decades; first in Arizona and since 1979 in Colorado where he joined the Solar Energy Research Institute (SERI) as a Senior Staff Member. In 1980, as Vice Chairman of the American Solar Energy Society, (ASES) he was General Chairman of its Solar Jubilee 25th Anniversary Meeting in Phoenix, attended by 1800 delegates.

He retired from SERI in 1984 but continues to consult for the Institute, which recently became the National Renewable Energy Laboratory. That same year, his 7th solar energy book, *Home Energy; Your Best Options for Solar Heating and Cooling, Wood Wind, and Photovoltaics,* was published by Rodale Press. In 1987 he served as Editor of the ASES magazine *Solar Today.*

In 1991, Dan attended the International Solar Energy Society's Solar World Congress in Denver, along with 1400 other delegates from around the world.

Order Form

Morning Sun Press - P.O. Box 413 - Lafayette, CA 94549
Phone & Fax (925) 932-1383

The Fuel Savers: A Kit of Solar Ideas for Your Home ($4.95)
by Bruce Anderson -paper, 83 pages, 5 x 8, 40 drawings, ISBN 0-9629069-0-5

Contains a wealth of ideas that can be easily adapted to almost any building.
From insulating curtains to solar hot water heaters, each idea is examined for
materials costs, fuel reduction, advantages and disadvantages, and cost-
effectiveness.
"A must for anyone interested in solar energy..." – New Age Retailer
*"A most practical step-by-step guide for individuals and homeowners to one of the
most important issues we face: reducing our wasteful dependence on fossil fuel."*
-- Paul Hawken

EarthScore: Your Personal Environmental Audit & Guide ($4.50)
by Donald Lotter -paper, 48 pages, 8 1/2 x 11with chart, ISBN 0-9629069-6-4

By analyzing 107 simple questions *EarthScore* takes you through a fun and
educational exercise and tallies Impact Points, which assess one's impact on
the environment; counts Action Points, measuring positive contributions, and
provides a score and rating on your own *EarthScore* Chart-- plus resources,
tips and suggestions are provided for immediate improvement.
*"A well-crafted guide to evaluating the impact of your actions on the earth and
scoring your earth-friendly quotient. A great motivator."*
Joe Dominguez and Vicki Robin, co-authors of *Your Money or Your Life*

Solar StoveTop Cooker Pattern ($12.00)
This pattern allows you to make the fascinating "reflector Cooker" which can
reach temperatures of 650 degrees F within minutes. It is the same cooker
described in *Cooking with the Sun* but all the figuring is done for you. All you
have to do is cut out the pattern, trace it onto cardboard and assemble the
pieces. Includes 28" x 42" pattern, instruction booklet with line drawings and
photos, resources and recipes.

Name_____
Address_____
City_____State_____Zip_____
Quantity:
_____ Cooking with the Sun: How to Build & Use Solar Cookers ($9.95)
_____ Solar StoveTop Cooker Pattern ($12.00)
_____ The Fuel Savers: A Kit of Solar Ideas for Your Home ($4.95)
_____ EarthScore: Your Personal Environmental Audit & Guide ($4.50)
Send a check or money order to: *Morning Sun Press, P.O. Box 413, Lafayette, CA
94549.* Phone/ fax (925) 932-1383. Add $2.00 for shipping and handling for the first
book and $.50 for each additional book. If you live in California add appropriate sales
tax. Quantity discounts available. Call, write or fax for details.